To Possess The Land

An Anthology of Confederation Poetry

Essential Anthologies Series 22

Guernica Editions Inc. acknowledges the support of the Canada Council for the Arts and the Ontario Arts Council. The Ontario Arts Council is an agency of the Government of Ontario.
We acknowledge the financial support of the Government of Canada.

To Possess The Land

An Anthology of Confederation Poetry

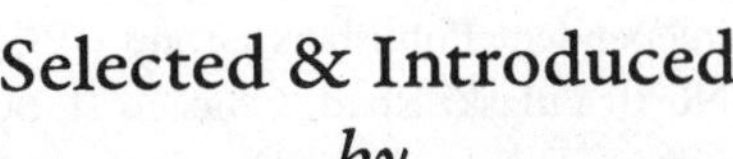

Selected & Introduced
by
JAMES DEAHL

GUERNICA EDITIONS
TORONTO • CHICAGO • BUFFALO • LANCASTER (U.K.)
2026

Guernica Founder, Antonio D'Alfonso

Michael Mirolla, editor
David Moratto, cover and interior design

Guernica Editions Inc.
1241 Marble Rock Rd., Gananoque (ON), Canada K7G 2V4
2250 Military Road, Tonawanda, N.Y. 14150-6000 U.S.A.
www.guernicaeditions.com

Distributors:
Independent Publishers Group (IPG)
600 North Pulaski Road, Chicago IL 60624
University of Toronto Press Distribution (UTP)
5201 Dufferin Street, Toronto (ON), Canada M3H 5T8

First edition.
Printed in Canada.

Legal Deposit—First Quarter
Library of Congress Catalog Card Number: 2025944392
Library and Archives Canada Cataloguing in Publication
Title: To possess the land : an anthology of Confederation poetry /
selected & introduced by James Deahl.
Names: Deahl, James, 1945- editor, writer of introduction
Series: Essential anthologies series ; 22.
Description: Series statement: Essential anthologies series ; 22
Identifiers: Canadiana 20250255332 | ISBN 9781778490170 (softcover)
Subjects: CSH: Canadian poetry (English)—19th century. |
CSH: Canadian poetry (English)—20th century. | LCGFT: Poetry.
Classification: LCC PS8289 .T6 2026 | DDC C811/.4080971—dc23

Dedicated to
my friend
Raymond Souster
People's Poet,
Publisher,
& Editor.

No poet did more
for our Confederation Poets,
for Canada,
and for poetry that
celebrates Canada.

Ultimately, we are what we are because we are where we are.
It was the first task for the Canadian imagination to possess the land.

—Malcolm Ross

CONTENTS

Introduction:
Our Confederation Poets 1
Editorial Note 5

Isabella Valancy Crawford. 7
8 poems from: The Collected Poems of Isabella Valancy Crawford (1905)
A Harvest Song 8
The Rose of a Nation's Thanks 9
The Camp of Souls 11
The Dark Stag 13
War 16
Peace 18
Toronto. 20
Said the West Wind. 22

George Frederick Cameron 25
8 poems from: Lyrics on Freedom, Love and Death (1887)
My Political Faith 26
Russia. 26
Erin 27
Standing On Tiptoe 28
Three Sonnets: On Leaving Nova Scotia, 1874 29
Sic Transit 30
Shelley 31
A Year After. 32

Barry Straton 35
6 poems from: Lays of Love, and Miscellaneous Poems (1884)
The Bloom on a Maiden's Cheek 36
Love's Harvest 37
America 38
Sunrise on the Ocean. 38
Sunset on the Ocean 40
Charity. 41
1 poem from: Songs of the Great Dominion: Voices from the Forests and Waters, the Settlements and Cities of Canada (1889)
A Dream Fulfilled. 43

Ethelwyn Wetherald 45
14 poems from: The Last Robin: Lyrics and Sonnets (1907)
April in the City 46
When It's Time for Leaves to Fly 46
Youth and Age 47
In Summer Rain. 47
The Sun in the Woods 48
The Song Sparrow's Nest 49
The Pasture Field 50
The Fields of Dark 51
A Midday in Midsummer. 52
The Prairie 53
Youth in Age 53
At Waking. 54
The Snow-fall. 54
The Silent Snow 55

William Douw Lighthall. 57
7 poems from: Old Measures: Collected Verse (1922)
Canada Not Last 58
The Caughnawaga Beadwork Seller 60
Winter's Dawn in Lower Canada 61
Deathless 62

To France 64
Commandant's Isle 64
Homer 66

S. Frances Harrison 69
5 poems from: Pine, Rose and Fleur de Lis (1890)
Nocturne 70
At St. Hilaire 70
Tintern Abbey 71
November 72
The Tree 73
3 poems from: In Northern Skies, And Other Poems (1912)
In March 75
The Marshes 77
At Valois 77

Wilfred Campbell 79
2 poems from: Snowflakes and Sunbeams (1888)
Indian Summer 80
On Christmas Eve 80
7 poems from: Lake Lyrics and Other Poems (1889)
Vapor and Blue 81
To the Lakes 82
Sunset, Lake Huron 83
The Tides of Dawn 84
Medwayosh 84
Alone 85
Infancy 86
1 poem from: The Dread Voyage (1893)
On a Summer Shore 86
4 poems from: Beyond the Hills of Dream (1899)
In the Spring Fields 88
Glory of the Dying Day 88
September in the Laurentian Hills 89
How One Winter Came in the Lake Region 90

2 poems from: The Poems of Wilfred Campbell (1905)
Cape Eternity 91
Death 92

Sir Charles G.D. Roberts 93
4 poems from: In Diverse Tones (1886)
Mist 94
Tantramar Revisited 94
The Potato Harvest 97
Tides 97
12 poems from: Songs of the Common Day and Ave!: An Ode for the Shelley Centenary (1893)
When Milking-Time is Done 98
The Salt Flats 98
The Pea-Fields 99
The Mowing 99
The Clearing 100
Buckwheat 100
In September 101
The Oat-Threshing 101
In an Old Barn 102
The Flight of the Geese 102
Blomidon 103
My Trees 103
5 poems from: The Book of the Native (1896)
Where the Cattle Come to Drink 104
An Epitaph for a Husbandman 104
The Stillness of the Frost 105
The Brook in February 106
Twilight on Sixth Avenue 106
1 poem from: New York Nocturnes And Other Poems (1898)
A Nocturne of Exile 107
1 poem from: The Book of the Rose (1903)
At the Wayside Shrine 108

John Frederic Herbin 111

14 poems from: The Marshlands and The Trail of the Tide (1899)

Across the Dykes 112
A Rifled Grave at Grand-Pré 112
The Sea-Harvest 113
In the Gaspereau Valley 113
The Broken Dyke 114
The Acadian Exile 114
A Homestead 115
Change 115
Restoration 118
The Tide-Line 119
Stone Ripple-Marks 119
To Minas 120
Blomidon 120
Seining 121

Helena Coleman 123

11 poems from: Songs and Sonnets (1906)

Give Me No Pity 124
I am Content with Canada 125
Love's Seasons 126
The Guardians of the Place 127
The Voices of Our Day 128
When Autumn Comes 128
Night Among the Thousand Islands 129
In October 130
At Sunset 131
Night 131
The Evening Hour 132

4 poems from: Marching Men: War Verses (1917)

The Day He Went 132
And They Were Young 133
Autumn, 1917 134
Convocation Hall 135

E. Pauline Johnson (Tekahionwake) 137
6 poems from: The White Wampum (1895)
As Red Men Die 138
A Cry from an Indian Wife. 140
Shadow River 142
Re-voyage 143
Brier. 145
Nocturne 145
7 poems from: Canadian Born (1903)
Harvest Time. 147
Low Tide at St. Andrews 148
Silhouette 148
The Sleeping Giant 149
At Crow's Nest Pass. 150
"Give Us Barabbas" 151
Fire-flowers 152
4 poems from: Flint and Feather (1912)
The Indian Corn Planter 152
The Cattle Country. 153
The Train Dogs 154
"And He Said, Fight On" 155

Frederick George Scott 157
16 poems from: Collected Poems (1934)
The Temple of the Ages 158
In the Winter Woods. 159
The Unnamed Lake 160
My Friend Death 162
Anniversary. 163
By the Grave of Keats 163
The Mill-stream 164
Shakespeare. 164
The Laurentians 165
A Grave in Flanders. 165
Quebec. 166

Requiescant 167
Winter 168
The Sea. 168
Out of the Storm 169
Last Post 169

Bliss Carman 171
5 poems from: Low Tide on Grand Pré: A Book of Lyrics (1893)
A Windflower 172
A Sea-Drift 172
A Northern Vigil 173
The Eavesdropper 176
The Vagabonds. 178
2 poems from: Ballads of Lost Haven: A Book of the Sea (1897)
Legends of Lost Haven. 181
The Shadow Boatswain 182
6 poems from: Later Poems (1921)
The Ships of Saint John 185
The Cry of the Hillborn. 187
Fireflies. 189
In October 189
The Ghost-yard of the Goldenrod. 190
Winter Twilight 191

Archibald Lampman. 193
4 poems from: Among the Millet, and Other Poems (1888)
Heat. 194
Among the Timothy 195
In October 198
Solitude 199
3 poems from: Lyrics of Earth (1895)
At the Ferry. 200
September 203
An Autumn Landscape 205

2 poems from: Alcyone, and Other Poems (1899)
Voices of Earth . . . 206
Winter Evening . . . 207
15 poems from: The Poems of Archibald Lampman (1900)
Beauty . . . 207
At Dusk . . . 208
A Sunset at Les Eboulements . . . 208
To a Millionaire . . . 209
The Modern Politician . . . 209
A January Morning . . . 210
A Forest Path in Winter . . . 210
After Mist . . . 211
In Beechwood Cemetery . . . 211
Goldenrod . . . 212
On Lake Temiscamingue . . . 212
Night in the Wilderness . . . 213
In the Wilds . . . 213
To the Ottawa . . . 214
Winter Uplands . . . 214

Duncan Campbell Scott . . . 217
4 poems from: New World Lyrics and Ballads (1905)
Rapids at Night . . . 219
Night Hymns on Lake Nipigon . . . 220
On the Way to the Mission . . . 221
The Wood Peewee . . . 223
2 poems from: Lundy's Lane, and Other Poems (1916)
The Height of Land . . . 224
Meditation at Perugia . . . 229
8 poems from: The Poems of Duncan Campbell Scott (1926)
Powassan's Drum . . . 231
September . . . 235
In the Country Churchyard . . . 235
The First Snow . . . 239
Watkwenies . . . 240

Off Riviere Du Loup 241
At Les Eboulements. 242
Night and the Pines. 242

Sophia M. Almon Hensley. 245
1 poem from: Poems (1889)
Noon 246
7 poems from: The Heart of a Woman (1906)
Consecrated. 247
At Ebb 247
The Turning of the Tide. 248
The Meaning of the Bird Song. 250
The Soul. 252
Returned. 253
Northwest Wind. 253
1 poem from: Canadian Poetry: From the Beginnings Through the First World War (1994)
Somewhere in France. 254

Textual Notes 255
Copy-Texts. 259
Bibliography 263
Acknowledgements 269
About the Editor. 271

Introduction:
Our Confederation Poets

No appreciation of the literature of the Confederation Period can ignore the central importance of the Bay of Fundy region of New Brunswick and Nova Scotia. During the final two decades of the nineteenth century, five writers developed a distinctive Canadian sensibility while rooted in the area. On the New Brunswick side of the vast bay, three cousins—Barry Straton, Sir Charles G.D. Roberts, and Bliss Carman—began writing poems about the striking landscape and rich social history of their home turf, especially the Tantramar Marshes. At the same time, two poets on the Nova Scotian side—the Acadian John Frederic Herbin and Sophia M. Almon Hensley—were doing much the same thing. Of the fifteen poets in this anthology who wrote about the Canadian landscape, one third were marked strongly by the Bay of Fundy and its sweeping marshlands. (The sole exception being George Frederick Cameron, who wrote no landscape poetry.)

And today, during the opening decades of the twenty-first century, many Canadians are continuing the tradition of our Confederation Poets. Just two of the notable poets working to celebrate the grandeur of the Fundy region are Allan Cooper and Margaret Patricia Eaton. While Québec and Ontario also possess rich histories and striking geographies, especially the Canadian Shield, the early roots of our literary culture are to be found in the Maritimes.

At the start of a truly Canadian poetry, our new nation had three regions: the Maritimes, Québec, and Ontario. While each had its own history and culture, there was a general vision—or a romantic *dream*—of what Canada was and of what it could be. Unfortunately, this vision was shattered initially by the First World War and, shortly thereafter, by the advent of Modernism. Therefore, the focus of this anthology will be on poetry published during the four decades between 1880 and 1920. After 1920 Canada was different; the War to End All Wars had changed everything. Nonetheless, it is crucial to understand what Canada was like during the final two decades of the nineteenth century and the first two decades of the twentieth century.

As already noted, all but one of the Confederation Poets wrote about Canada's geography, climate, and history. They wanted to describe their newly minted nation. It was a period of optimism. These poets were generally forward looking, not backward looking. To them, the future offered exciting possibilities for Canada. In this endeavour, they often looked to William Wordsworth (1770–1850) and the other British Lake District Poets. This was a time of Romanticism in England, and this feeling permeated our Confederation Poets.

At the beginning of the nineteenth century, British poetry was highly Romantic. First, there were poets like Wordsworth and Coleridge and, shortly thereafter, Keats and Shelley. And while our Confederation Poets were writing at the *close* of the nineteenth century when Romanticism was passing in England, the Romantic spirit still held a powerful allure for them. Wilfred Campbell strove greatly to create a "Lake Region" in Ontario. If Wordsworth could be the poet of the Lake District, Campbell would be the poet of our own Lake Region (the Lake Huron-Georgian Bay-Bruce Peninsula area of the Great Lakes).

This is not to suggest that our poets slavishly copied Wordsworth and the other followers of Romanticism across the water. England has nothing like the Canadian Shield. (And all of Britain has nothing like the stern but vibrant beauty of Canada's northland, except for the Highlands of Scotland.) Rather, they tried to do for Canada what Wordsworth and his fellow nature poets had done so well for England. They wanted to show that Canada was *not* England by using concrete descriptions. The result was often a picture of Canada that was, to one degree or another, romanticized. In fact, this amalgam of Romanticism and realism is the hallmark of much of the early poetry of the Confederation Period. As Canada moved deeper into the twentieth century, the romance of the initial dream began to fade, and no group of poets could halt that process.

One of the lasting gifts of our poets was to imprint a vision of Canada in our national imagination that future generations of writers would use as a foundation. Thus, the Maritime Region holds a special place in our hearts, even for Canadians who have never visited Nova Scotia or New Brunswick or seen the Tantramar Marshes. And the same holds true for the Canadian Shield in Québec and Ontario.

These poets were not solely nature poets; most addressed other topics. Indeed, their poetry is richly varied in both form and content. Just like poets today, the Confederation Poets were influenced by the social and political issues of their time. Several of the women included here were early feminists. Others were concerned about the "too close" relationship Canada had developed with the United States and the weakening of the tie to England. They distrusted Americanization and wanted to remain within the British Empire (now Commonwealth).

But it is not for me, the editor, to tell you, the reader, what these poets had to say or what to think about them. Readers of *To Possess The Land* should make up their own minds about the Confederation Period, the culture these poets represented, and what each contributed to the Canada we have today. So, read on.

Editorial Note

The reader might wonder why many of the most important poems from the Confederation Period are not included in this anthology. Poems such as Archibald Lampman's "The City of the End of Things," E. Pauline Johnson's "The Song My Paddle Sings," Bliss Carman's "Low Tide on Grand Pré," Isabella Valancy Crawford's "The Lily Bed," and Helena Coleman's "When First He Put the Khaki On," along with fifty other seminal pieces are quoted in full in *The Confederation Poets: The Founding of a Canadian Poetry, 1880 to the First World War*, also published by Guernica Editions.

My rule is to not have the same poem appear in both books. And because we know that "the exception proves the rule," my sole exception is "Indian Summer" by Wilfred Campbell because it is the best-loved Confederation poem today.

My decision is to always quote each poem, if possible, from the version last published during the poet's lifetime. Therefore, Wilfred Campbell's "Indian Summer" is quoted from *The Poems of Wilfred Campbell* (1905), although it first appeared in his *Snowflakes and Sunbeams* (1888). Likewise, Sir Charles G.D. Roberts' "The Tantramar Revisited" was initially published in *In Diverse Tones* (1886), but my copy-text is "Tantramar Revisited" as it appears in *Poems: New Complete Edition* (1907). Sir Charles made a few changes to his poem for his 1907 collection.

Each poet's section is introduced by a short biographical note. These have been kept brief because each of these sixteen poets is discussed more fully in the companion volume, *The Confederation Poets*. Many readers will notice that some poems mentioned as being of major significance in these notes do not, in fact, appear in this anthology. Just two examples are Ethelwyn Wetherald's "Hester Prynne Speaks" and "Evening on the Marshes" by Barry Straton. These poems, and many others, are presented in full in the companion volume.

Isabella Valancy Crawford

Unlike the other Confederation Poets in this anthology, all of whom were Canadian born, Isabella Valancy Crawford was born on December 25, 1850 in Dublin, Ireland. Our poet moved to Paisley, Ontario, where her father had established a medical practice, with her mother and siblings at the age of seven. At that time, Paisley was a frontier village in the backwoods of Canada West. When she was about the age of puberty, the Crawford family moved to Lakefield, a village in Ontario's Kawartha Lakes area. And later her family would move again to Peterborough, where Dr. Crawford died.

Although Crawford started to publish her early poetry while still in Peterborough, she wrote almost all of her major work in Toronto, where she relocated with her mother soon after the death of her father. She would keep her childhood close, and the frontier would remain a vital part of her literary imagination for the rest of her life, despite living her final years in Toronto. Sadly, Crawford died young on February 12, 1887. Her standard text, *The Collected Poems of Isabella Valancy Crawford*, edited by J.W. Garvin in 1905, was published eighteen years following the poet's death. Even though Isabella Valancy Crawford died in poverty and obscurity, she remains among the leading poets of her era.

A Harvest Song

The noon was as a crystal bowl
The red wine mantled through;
Around it like a Viking's beard
The red-gold hazes blew,
As tho' he quaffed the ruddy draught
While swift his galley flew.

This mighty Viking was the Night;
He sailed about the earth,
And called the merry harvest-time
To sing him songs of mirth;
And all on earth or in the sea
To melody gave birth.

The valleys of the earth were full
To rocky lip and brim
With golden grain that shone and sang
When woods were still and dim,
A little song from sheaf to sheaf—
Sweet Plenty's cradle-hymn.

O gallant were the high tree-tops,
And gay the strain they sang!
And cheerfully the moon-lit hills
Their echo-music rang!
And what so proud and what so loud
As was the ocean's clang!

But O the little humming song
That sang among the sheaves!
'Twas grander than the airy march
That rattled thro' the leaves,
And prouder, louder, than the deep,
Bold clanging of the waves:

"The lives of men, the lives of men
With every sheaf are bound!
We are the blessing which annuls
The curse upon the ground!
And he who reaps the Golden Grain
The Golden Love hath found."

The Rose of a Nation's Thanks

A welcome? Oh, yes, 'tis a kindly word, but why will they plan and prate
Of feasting and speeches and such small things, while the wives and mothers wait?
Plan as ye will, and do as ye will, but think of the hunger and thirst
In the hearts that wait; and do as ye will, but lend us our laddies first!
Why, what would ye have? There is not a lad that treads in the gallant ranks
Who does not already bear on his breast the Rose of a Nation's Thanks!

A welcome? Why, what do you mean by that, when the very stones must sing
As our men march over them home again; the walls of the city ring
With the thunder of throats and the tramp and tread of feet that rush and run?—
I think in my heart that the very trees must shout for the bold work done!
Why, what would ye have? There is not a lad that treads in the gallant ranks
Who does not already bear on his breast the Rose of a Nation's Thanks!

A welcome? There is not a babe at the breast won't spring at the roll of the drum
That heralds them home—the keen, long cry in the air of "They come! They come!"
And what of it all if ye bade them wade knee-deep in a wave of wine,
And tossed tall torches, and arched the town in garlands of maple and pine?
All dust in the wind of a woman's cry as she snatches from the ranks
Her boy who bears on his bold young breast the Rose of a Nation's Thanks!

A welcome? There's a doubt if the lads would stand like stone in their steady line
When a babe held high on a dear wife's hand or the stars that swim and shine
In a sweetheart's eyes, or a mother's smile, flashed far in the welded crowd,
Or a father's proud voice, half-sob and half-cheer, cried on a son aloud.
O the billows of waiting hearts that swelled would sweep from the martial ranks
The gallant boys who bear on their breasts the Rose of a Nation's Thanks!

A welcome? O Joy, can they stay your feet, or measure the wine of your bliss?
O Joy, let them have you alone to-day—a day with a pulse like this!
A welcome? Yes, 'tis a tender thought, a green laurel that laps the sword—
But Joy has the wing of a wild white swan, and the song of a free wild bird!
She must beat the air with her wing at will, at will must her song be driven

From her heaving heart and tremulous throat through the
 awful arch of heaven.
And what would ye have? There isn't a lad will burst from
 the shouting ranks
But bears like a star on his faded coat the Rose of a Nation's
 Thanks!

The Camp of Souls

My white canoe, like the silvery air
 O'er the River of Death that darkly rolls
When the moons of the world are round and fair,
 I paddle back from the "Camp of Souls."
When the wishton-wish in the low swamp grieves
Come the dark plumes of red "Singing Leaves."

Two hundred times have the moons of spring
 Rolled over the bright bay's azure breath
Since they decked me with plumes of an eagle's wing,
 And painted my face with the "paint of death,"
And from their pipes o'er my corpse there broke
The solemn rings of the blue "last smoke."

Two hundred times have the wintry moons
 Wrapped the dead earth in a blanket white;
Two hundred times have the wild sky loons
 Shrieked in the flush of the golden light
Of the first sweet dawn, when the summer weaves
Her dusky wigwam of perfect leaves.

Two hundred moons of the falling leaf
 Since they laid my bow in my dead right hand
And chanted above me the "song of grief"
 As I took my way to the spirit land;
Yet when the swallow the blue air cleaves
Come the dark plumes of red "Singing Leaves."

White are the wigwams in that far camp,
    And the star-eyed deer on the plains are found;
No bitter marshes or tangled swamp
    In the Manitou's happy hunting-ground!
And the moon of summer forever rolls
Above the red men in their "Camp of Souls."

Blue are its lakes as the wild dove's breast,
    And their murmurs soft as her gentle note;
As the calm, large stars in the deep sky rest,
    The yellow lilies upon them float;
And canoes, like flakes of the silvery snow,
Thro' the tall, rustling rice-beds come and go.

Green are its forests; no warrior wind
    Rushes on war trail the dusk grove through,
With leaf-scalps of tall trees mourning behind;
    But South Wind, heart friend of Great Manitou,
When ferns and leaves with cool dews are wet,
Blows flowery breaths from his red calumet.

Never upon them the white frosts lie,
    Nor glow their green boughs with the "paint of death";
Manitou smiles in the crystal sky,
    Close breathing above them His life-strong breath;
And He speaks no more in fierce thunder sound,
So near is His happy hunting-ground.

Yet often I love, in my white canoe,
    To come to the forests and camps of earth:
'Twas there death's black arrow pierced me through;
    'Twas there my red-browed mother gave me birth;
There I, in the light of a young man's dawn,
Won the lily heart of dusk "Springing Fawn."

And love is a cord woven out of life,
And dyed in the red of the living heart;
And time is the hunter's rusty knife,
That cannot cut the red strands apart:
And I sail from the spirit shore to scan
Where the weaving of that strong cord began.

But I may not come with a giftless hand,
So richly I pile, in my white canoe,
Flowers that bloom in the spirit land,
Immortal smiles of Great Manitou.
When I paddle back to the shores of earth
I scatter them over the white man's hearth.

For love is the breath of the soul set free;
So I cross the river that darkly rolls,
That my spirit may whisper soft to thee
Of *thine* who wait in the "Camp of Souls."
When the bright day laughs, or the wan night grieves,
Come the dusky plumes of red "Singing Leaves."

The Dark Stag

A startled stag, the blue-grey Night,
Leaps down beyond black pines.
Behind—a length of yellow light—
The hunter's arrow shines:
His moccasins are stained with red,
He bends upon his knee,
From covering peaks his shafts are sped,
The blue mists plume his mighty head,—
Well may the swift Night flee!

The pale, pale Moon, a snow-white doe,
  Bounds by his dappled flank:
They beat the stars down as they go,
  Like wood-bells growing rank.
The winds lift dewlaps from the ground,
  Leap from the quaking reeds;
Their hoarse bays shake the forests round,
With keen cries on the track they bound,—
  Swift, swift the dark stag speeds!

Away! his white doe, far behind,
  Lies wounded on the plain;
Yells at his flank the nimblest wind,
  His large tears fall in rain;
Like lily-pads, small clouds grow white
  About his darkling way;
From his bald nest upon the height
The red-eyed eagle sees his flight;
He falters, turns, the antlered Night,—
  The dark stag stands at bay!

His feet are in the waves of space;
  His antlers broad and dun
He lowers; he turns his velvet face
  To front the hunter, Sun;
He stamps the lilied clouds, and high
  His branches fill the west.
The lean stork sails across the sky,
The shy loon shrieks to see him die,
  The winds leap at his breast.

Roar the rent lakes as thro' the wave
   Their silver warriors plunge,
As vaults from core of crystal cave
   The strong, fierce muskellunge;
Red torches of the sumach glare,
   Fall's council-fires are lit;
The bittern, squaw-like, scolds the air;
The wild duck splashes loudly where
   The rustling rice-spears knit.

Shaft after shaft the red Sun speeds:
   Rent the stag's dappled side,
His breast, fanged by the shrill winds, bleeds,
   He staggers on the tide;
He feels the hungry waves of space
   Rush at him high and blue;
Their white spray smites his dusky face,
Swifter the Sun's fierce arrows race
   And pierce his stout heart thro'.

His antlers fall; once more he spurns
   The hoarse hounds of the day;
His blood upon the crisp blue burns,
   Reddens the mounting spray;
His branches smite the wave—with cries
   The loud winds pause and flag—
He sinks in space—red glow the skies,
The brown earth crimsons as he dies,
   The strong and dusky stag.

War

Shake, shake the earth with giant tread,
Thou red-maned Titan bold;
For every step a man lies dead,
A cottage hearth is cold.
Take up the babes with mailèd hands,
Transfix them with thy spears,
Spare not the chaste young virgin-bands,
Tho' blood may be their tears.

Beat down the corn, tear up the vine,
The waters turn to blood;
And if the wretch for bread doth whine,
Give him his kin for food.
Ay, strew the dead to saddle-girth,
They makė so rich a mold,
Thou wilt enrich the wasted earth—
They'll turn to yellow gold.

On with thy thunders! Shot and shell
Send screaming, featly hurled—
Science has made them in her cell
To *civilize* the world.
Not, not alone where Christian men
Pant in the well-armed strife,
But seek the jungle-throttled glen—
The savage has a life!

He has a soul—so priests will say—
Go, save it with thy sword!
Thro' his rank forests force thy way,
Thy war cry, "For the Lord!"
Rip up his mines, and from his strands
Wash out the gold with blood—
Religion raises blessing hands,
"War's evil worketh good!"

When striding o'er the conquered land
Silence thy rolling drum,
And, led by white-robed choiring band,
With loud "*Te Deum*" come.
Seek the grim chancel, on its wall
Thy blood-stiff banner hang;
They lie who say thy blood is gall,
Thy tooth the serpent's fang.

See, the white Christ is lifted high,
Thy conquering sword to bless!
Smiles the pure Monarch of the sky—
Thy king can do no less.
Drink deep with him the festal wine,
Drink with him drop for drop;
If like the sun his throne doth shine,
Of it *thou* art the prop.

If spectres wait upon the bowl,
Thou needst not be afraid;
Grim hell-hounds for thy bold, black soul,
His purple be thy shade.
Go, feast with Commerce, be her spouse!
She loves thee, thou art hers;
For thee she decks her board and house,
Then how may others curse

If she, mild-seeming matron, leans
Upon thine iron neck,
And leaves with thee her household scenes
To follow at thy beck?
Bastard in brotherhood of kings,
Their blood runs in thy veins;
For them the crowns; the sword that swings
For thee, to hew their chains.

For thee the rending of the prey;
  They, jackals to the lion,
Tread after in the gory way
  Trod by the mightier scion.
O slave, that slayest other slaves,
  O'er vassals crowned a king,
O War, build high thy throne with graves,
  High as the vulture's wing!

Peace

Peace stands within the city wall;
Most like a god she towers tall,
And bugle-like she cries to all.

In place of sounds of nether hell,
In place of serpent hiss of shell,
Sounds sweet her powerful "All's well!"

Is she a willow by a stream?
The spirit of a dreamer's dream?
The pale moon's meek and phantom beam?

The mere desire of panting soul?
Water, not wine, within the bowl?
Rides she, a ghost, upon the roll

Of spectral seas? Nay, see her rise,
Strong flesh against the flushing skies,
Large calm within her watchful eyes.

The olive darkling o'er her face,
Like one of Caryæ's sculptured race,
Her arms uphold the nation's place.

Like ivory beams, her strong white feet
Span over all the busy street;
Beneath their arch the merchants meet.

Her eyes are terrible and pure
As the stern, steadfast cynosure;
Before them bow and bend the poor.

Their thrilling pæans rise to her;
She mothers all the healthy stir
That beats the air with bruit and birr.

Below her feet War's banners furl,
The bounteous palms about her curl,
Above her head her strong doves whirl.

Her vesture, with giant lilies bound,
Falls like a slant of snow, and round
It whitens all the quiet ground.

Its cloven fringes are of gold;
By her vast calm made brave and bold,
Babes by their summer lightnings hold.

A helmet binds her lofty crest;
Strong scales of steel flash on her vest,
A strong shield on her ample breast.

Armed, armed she stands, from head to heel;
Afar strange navies meet and reel;
Far sounds the furious clash of steel.

Around her sounds the reaper's song,
Below her moves the busy throng;
So stands she—terrible and strong.

Ardent and awfully, afar
Blazes the blood-red wand'ring star
That rolls before the feet of war;

But wheels not nigh her sentried gate,
Her sinewed battlements that wait
Panting to guard her lofty state.

Her song is mild, but thro' it still
The blast of bugles, stern and shrill,
The calms about her pierce and thrill.

Armed, armed her head, her foot, her breast,
A spear defends her white dove's nest;
As Peace is strong so is she blest.

Toronto

She moves to meet the centuries, her feet
All shod with emerald, and her light robe
Fringed with leaves singing in the jazel air.
Her tire is rich, not with stout battlements,
Prophets of strife, but wealthy with tall spires
All shining Godward, rare with learning's domes,
And burning with young stars that promise suns
To clasp her older brows. On her young breast
Lie linked the fair, clear pearls of many homes,—
Mighty and lovely chain, from its white strength
Hangs on her heart the awful jewel, Hope.

She moves to meet the centuries, nor lies
All languid waiting, with the murmuring kiss
Of the large waters on white, nerveless feet,
And dim, tranced gaze upon the harbour bar,

And dusk, still boughs knit over her prone head,
And rose-soft hands that idly pluck the turf,
And rose lips singing idly thro' her dream.

She hears the marching centuries which Time
Leads up the dark peaks of Eternity:
The pulses of past warriors bound in her;
The pulses of dead sages beat in her;
The pulses of dead merchants stir in her;
The roses of her young feet turn to flame,
Yet ankle-deep in tender buds of spring;
Till, with the perfumes of close forests thick
Upon her tender flesh, she to her lips
Lifts the bold answering trump, and, winding shrill
With voices of her people and her waves
Notes of quick joy, half queen, half child, she bounds
To meet the coming Time, and climbs the steps
Of the tall throne he builds upon her strand.

Toronto, joy and peace! When comes the day
Close domes of marble rich with gold leap up
From porphyry pillars to the eye-clear sky,
And when the wealthy fringes of thy robe
Sweep outward league on league, and to thee come
The years all bowed with treasures for thy house,
On lusty shoulders, still remember thee
Of thy first cradle on the lilies' lap
In the dim woods; and tho' thy diadem
Make a new sunrise, still, amid its flame,
Twine for the nursing lilies' sake the glow
Of God-like lilies round about thy brows—
Honour and Peace and sweet-breathed Charity!

Said the West Wind

I love old earth! Why should I lift my wings,
My misty wings, so high above her breast
That flowers would shake no perfumes from their hearts,
And waters breathe no whispers to the shores?
I love deep places builded high with woods,
Deep, dusk, fern-closed, and starred with nodding blooms,
Close watched by hills, green, garlanded and tall.

On hazy wings, all shot with mellow gold,
I float, I float thro' shadows clear as glass;
With perfumed feet I wander o'er the seas,
And touch white sails with gentle finger-tips;
I blow the faithless butterfly against
The rose-red thorn, and thus avenge the rose;
I whisper low amid the solemn boughs,
And stir a leaf where not my loudest sigh
Could move the emerald branches from their calm,—
Leaves, leaves, I love ye much, for ye and I
Do make sweet music over all the earth!

I dream by glassy ponds, and, lingering, kiss
The gold crowns of their lilies one by one,
As mothers kiss their babes who be asleep
On the clear gilding of their infant heads,
Lest if they kissed the dimple on the chin,
The rose flecks on the cheek or dewy lips,
The calm of sleep might feel the touch of love,
And so be lost. I steal before the rain,
The longed-for guest of summer; as his fringe
Of mist drifts slowly from the mountain peaks,
The flowers dance to my fairy pipe and fling
Rich odours on my wings, and voices cry,
"The dear West Wind is damp, and rich with scent;
We shall have fruits and yellow sheaves for this."

At night I play amid the silver mists,
And chase them on soft feet until they climb
And dance their gilded plumes against the stars;
At dawn the last round primrose star I hide
By wafting o'er her some small fleck of cloud,
And ere it passes comes the broad, bold Sun
And blots her from the azure of the sky,
As later, toward his noon, he blots a drop
Of pollen-gilded dew from violet cup
Set bluely in the mosses of the wood.

George Frederick Cameron

George Frederick Cameron was born on September 24, 1854 in New Glasgow, Nova Scotia, and died a week before his thirty-first birthday on September 17, 1885 at Millhaven, Ontario. Because of his untimely death, Cameron did not have time to assemble a book-length manuscript of his poetry. This task fell to his brother, Charles J. Cameron. Cameron's standard text, *Lyrics on Freedom, Love and Death,* was published two years following the poet's death.

Although he died so young, Cameron studied law in Boston, practiced law in that city for five years, returned to Canada to study at Queen's University in Kingston, and served as editor of that city's *Daily News.* Unlike the other fifteen poets in this anthology, Cameron wrote no nature poetry—he was chiefly a poet of ideas and emotions—and his only poem about his birthplace is "Three Sonnets: On Leaving Nova Scotia, 1874."

My Political Faith

I am not of those fierce, wild wills,
   Albeit from loins of warlike line,
   To wreck laws human and divine
Alike, that on a million ills
   I might erect one sacred shrine

To Freedom: nor again am I
   Of *these* who could be sold and bought
   To fall before a Juggernaut:
I hold all "royal right" a lie—
   Save that a royal soul hath wrought!

It is in the extreme begins
   And ends all danger: if the Few
   Would feel, or if the Many knew
This fact, the mass of fewer sins
   Would shrive them in their passing through:

O'er all God's footstool not a slave
   Should under his great glory stand,
   For men would rise, swift sword in hand,
And give each tyrant to his grave
   And freedom to each lovely land.

Russia

There Russia lightless land of pain,
   Rude region of forbidden thought,
Where Freedom, walking, clanks a chain,
   Or pines in prison till she rot:—

Where every moment breaks a heart,
  Where hope can hardly draw a breath,
Where rumbles still the hangman's cart,
  And all the air is thick with death:—

Yea, Russia—sick and sad of soul,
  And, like the camel, forced to kneel,
Feels on her back the burden roll,
  And lifts again the old appeal;

And vainly lifts it: while the throng
  Of maid, and woman, man and child,
Goes outward—singing sadder song
  Than Babel's—to Siberia's wild.

But even for *thee* there is a hope,—
  That better Ruler shall be thine,
Whose sway shall show that cell, and rope,
  Are not the seals of "Right Divine."

This failing thee—a Power shall wake
  As stern as steel, as strong as stone;
A Power that never fails to shake
  A *too-dark* Despot from his throne:—

Rebellion's self, with vengeful hand,
  Disdaining civic wreath and robe,
Shall take the sword, and blazing brand,
  And sweep the Gorgon from the globe.

Erin

Here Ireland, stricken, begs for balms,
  For broken heart and bruised flesh;
Still shows the nail-prints in her palms
  And cries, being crucified afresh.

And, 'twixt the fools who hate her most,
    And those who hurt her most—her own,
She has but little left to boast
    Save strength to struggle on alone,

And courage still to persevere
    In what she holds her right divine,
And faith to feel that *some* New Year
    Shall see her star of promise shine:

And so it shall! The season hastes
    O Erin, when the last of woes
Shall come to thee, and all thy wastes
    Shall bloom and blossom as the rose!

January 1st, 1884

Standing On Tiptoe

Standing on tiptoe ever since my youth
    Striving to grasp the future just above,
I hold at length the only future—Truth,
    And Truth is Love.

I feel as one who being awhile confined
    Sees drop to dust about him all his bars:—
The clay grows less, and, leaving it, the mind
    Dwells with the stars.

Sept. 1885

Three Sonnets: On Leaving Nova Scotia, 1874

I

Farewell! And I must speak the word to-day;
And I must leave what I have known so long,—
And only known to love, and loved to know!
The breeze moves strongly outward from the bay,—
And here and there amid the busy throng
Affection wrings the hands of those who go,
And love as deep the hearts of those who stay.
The feast is o'er, and sad the parting song!
Why not? These hills our feet have trod in youth:
Why not? These vales our earliest vision knew:
Why not? These friends—we long have prov'n their truth:
And now to each and all we bid adieu!
The lines are cast: loud rings the warning bell:
Swift clasp of hands, brief kiss,—and long farewell!

II

I stand alone at midnight on the deck,
And watch with eager eye the sinking shore
Which I may view, it may be, nevermore:
For there is tempest, battle, fire, and wreck,
And ocean hath her share of each of these,—
Attest it, thousand rotting argosies,
Wealth-laden, sunken in the southern seas!
And who can say that evermore these feet
Shall tread thy soil, Acadia? Who can say
That evermore this heart of mine shall greet
The loved to whom it sighs adieu to-day?
Our sail is set for countries far away;
Our sail is set, and now is no retreat,
Though Ocean should but lure, like Beauty, to betray!

III

When shall I see them all again? I say,
  Now that the loved, lost land lies far a-lea,—
Now that we are upon the world's highway,
  Now that we are alone upon the sea.
When shall I meet them all, when shall it be?
  When shall I come to them, if ever? When
Shall I come back to these dear ones again?
Speak, ocean-winds! Is it beyond your ken?
  When shall I come to them, or they to me?
I hear no tone; no token gives the wind:
  The only voice is where above the shrouds
The sea-mew screams defiance to the clouds:
  Till Night comes down, about, before, behind,
And locks all lands from sight, but locks not mine from mind!

Sic Transit

A noble record! so he said in pride,
  A noble record, and right nobly won,
  Which ages yet to be shall look upon;
A noble record! so he said—and died.
And, lo! the years came up from out the sea
  Of time; like dreams all old things passed away—
  The bud that gave rich promise yesterday
Of fair and fragrant immortality
  Dropped faded, withered—ceased for aye to be,—
And with it died the poet's proudest lay.

Shelley

I

"Dust unto dust?" No, spirit unto spirit
For thee, beloved! for thou wert all fire,
All luminous flame, all passionate desire,
All things that mighty beings do inherit,
All things that mighty beings do require.
"Dust unto dust?" Ah, no! Thou did'st respire
In such a high and holy atmosphere,
Where clouds are not, but calms, and all things clear,—
Not one like ours, but purer far and higher,—
Thou did'st not know of dust. How "dust to dust" then here?

II

Spirit to spirit, be it! Thou wert born
An heir apparent to the throne of mind.
It lessens not thy right that some were blind,
And looked on thee and fixt a lip of scorn,
And threw on thee the venom of their kind:
Thou wert a brother to the sun and wind,
And it is meet that thou art of them now.
I see thee standing, with thy godlike brow
High-arched and star-lit, upwardly inclined,
While at thy feet the singers of sweet song do bow.

III

For spirits are not as men: *these* did not know
An angel had been with them on the earth,—
A singer who had caused a glorious birth
Of glorious after-singers here below,—
Where much was sung and little sung of worth.
I see the stars about thee as a girth,—

The moon in splendor standing by thy side,
And lesser moons that evermore do glide
About her circling, making songs of mirth,—
And o'er thy head supreme Apollo in his pride,—

IV

Pleased with the homage that his children give thee,
Remembering it as *his*, even as thou art;
Knowing thy heart a portion of his heart,
And spreading forth his breast as to receive thee—
Twin soul of his, that had been rent apart.
I leave to marts the language of the mart.
Ashes to ashes say above the crust
Of him who *was* but ashes,—it is just!
But over *thee* as homeward thou did'st start,
Spirit to spirit was true, and not "dust unto dust!"

March 21st, 1883

A Year After

A Sonnet

Who of us thought upon that gay May night,—
That night of joy, and jollity, and cheer,—
That two, within the circle of a year,
Two of our number should have passed from sight—
Passed from this present to another sphere,—
Passed through death's darkness out into life's light?
Not one of us now living. Happy all,
We wished not morn, nor sighed for yesterday:
We gave no thought to funeral pomp or pall,
Or gnawing worm, or darkness, or decay.

Yet are they gone: and we, who yet remain,
    Grasp but this lesson: it is ever thus,—
Though pleasure drown awhile all thought of pain,
Though we forget of death, yet Death forgets not us.

Boston

Barry Straton

The eldest of three poetic cousins, Barry Bliss Straton was born on December 27, 1854 in Fredericton, New Brunswick. Straton became the first poet to celebrate the beauty of the Bay of Fundy's Tantramar Marshes when his poem "Evening on the Marshes" was published in 1884 in his poetry collection, *Lays of Love, and Miscellaneous Poems*. Sadly, he never published a second collection because he died on October 10, 1901 in Maugerville Parish, New Brunswick.

The three poets were close, and it seems likely that Straton's "Evening on the Marshes" influenced his younger cousins, Sir Charles G.D. Roberts and Bliss Carman, when it came to writing about the marshlands and the people who lived and worked there. Like his cousins, he attended the Fredericton Collegiate School, where they were influenced by the ideas of Sir George Robert Parkin. But unlike Roberts and Carman, he took a different road and chose farming instead of university. *Lays of Love* contains several fine poems, and his "Evening on the Marshes" helped establish the Fundean Marshlands in Canadian Literature.

The Bloom on a Maiden's Cheek

Sweet hours I whiled with a maiden meek,
When the golden sun sought the crimson west,
Where the lilies rest on the mirroring stream,
And blushing to see their beauty, seem
Like the bloom on a maiden's cheek.

The whip-poor-will sang to the laughing creek,
The butterfly hid in her nest for the night,
As the golden light through the tree-tops rushed,
And kissed the stream till its wavelets flushed
Like the bloom on a maiden's cheek.

The red moon rose o'er the purple peak,
And chasing the sun from the western sky,
Sent her bright rays high to the stars' abode,
And bathed the clouds till their edges glowed
Like the bloom on a maiden's cheek.

. . . .

I sought the dell in the autumn bleak.
The cold, dark clouds threw a gloom on the day,
The warblers gay from their nests had flown,
The sweet red rose from the bank had gone
Like the bloom from the maiden's cheek.

The north wind blew with a dismal shriek,
The brown cones fell from the boughs overhead,
The lily lay dead in the breast of the stream,
From the brooklet's wave had passed the gleam
Like the bloom from the maiden's cheek.

Ah! never again in merry freak
Shall we roam at eve in the golden light.
All the blossoms bright are below the snow,
From the western sky has passed the glow
And the bloom from the maiden's cheek.

Love's Harvest

The furrows of life Time is plowing,
    But we mourn not the Spring which departs,
For the husbandman Fate, in his sowing,
    Scattered love in the soil of our hearts.

The sunshine of virtue and beauty
    Shall wake the sweet seedlings to bloom.
The warm dews of mercy and duty
    Shall moisten the tractable loam.

Oh, blow, grains of love to the binding!
    Oh, blush, golden fruit on the hill!
'Tis a dreary, long day to the grinding,
    But a short, pleasant way from the mill.

But fondness and faith will be growing,
    Be the sky clear or cloudy above.
When fortune is ripe to my mowing
    We shall gather our harvest of love!

America

Sonnet

Columbus came to thee and called thee new!
New World to him, but thy rich blood, bright gold,
Lay cold where once the fires manifold
Raged fiercely. New? Primeval forests grew,
Had fallen, and were coal! Thine eagles flew
Undaunted then as now, and where the bold
South Rocky Mountains rise in fold on fold
The Aztec to his God the victim slew.
The tropic verdure of thy far north world
Had passed for ever, moon-like fading out.
Sky-piercing mounts have reared them from the seas—
The lost Atlantis has been depth-ward hurled,
Since thou wert new!—Old! all thy landmarks shout,
And bid us read thy waiting mysteries.

Sunrise on the Ocean

I stand beside the sleeping Sea
To view the morn. The shades of night
Rise from its bosom silently.
The golden light from out the Gate
Of Heaven streams and takes its flight
O'er wakening wave and whispering beach.
As far as eager eye can reach,
O'er verdant isle and mirroring strait,
The soft refulgence falls and glows.
The sunrays break across the sea;
O'er mountain, meadow, lake and lea
The rich light leaps, and sweeps, and flows,
Till all the swelling radiancy
Springs perfect in a new-born day.

Along the Ocean's level tide
The pale mists glide and flee the sun.
Like midnight phantoms, swift they run
Before the searching day and hide
Far down the west. From rest the waves
Awake and shake their robes of foam
Beneath the glorious morning sky,
And sparkling in the sunbeams, roam
To whisper in resounding caves
Weird notes of Neptune's melody.

Fresh from the darksome realms of night
The breezes ruff the Ocean's breast;
The slumbering vessels start from rest
And spread their lofty sails of white.
Oh! safely, swiftly wing the seas,
Ye lonesome wanderers o'er the deep,
Below whose ways vast navies sleep,
And bear to waiting native quays
The rich returns from crowded marts,
The sun-born fruits of tropic lands,
The regal gifts of golden strands,
The loves of constant, longing hearts.

Who knows the dangers of the deep—
The ships that go, but never come—
The widowed hearts that wait and weep—
The missing sunshine of the home—
The stalwart forms—the honest hands
That grace no more their natal lands—
The thunder's crash—the lightning's glare—
The wrack upon the middle seas—
The famine and the wild despair,—
The sweetest gift that reason flees,—
May hold our hardy sailors brave,
May breathe a prayer such lives to save.

The glowing sun mounts high in air!
Come! Flee his burning rays that fall,
And in some shady grotto, where
The droning waves break dreamily,
And faintly floats the sea-mew's call,
Recount strange lays of hoary sea.

Sunset on the Ocean

The sun has made the sea his bed.
  In gold and red arrayed, the West
Shines as if Heaven's portal bright
Were oped to cast immortal light
    Upon the Ocean's breast.

The sapphire waves through coral sweep;
  The mermaids leap from caves below;
Lulled on the kissing wavelet's crest,
They sing with harps to bosoms prest
    Beneath the sunset's glow.

From wind-kissed lips of purling foam
  Sweet echoes roam, and tips of waves
Weave golden snakes and flakes of flame
To light the merry mermen's game,
    And gild the deep sea-caves.

The sea-mew wings the breathing air,
  And half in fear he sings his call,
As over such enchanted seas
To reach his mate he quickly flees,
    While twilight shadows fall.

The mists of night like ghosts arise,
And from the skies the light erase.
With one long sigh in sympathy,
We homeward turn, O mystic sea,
With solemn, lingering pace.

Charity

Come! walk with the world and go down to the destitute homes of the poor,
Where weeping is louder than laughter, where sorrow and famine abide;
Where Azrael reaps a full harvest and darkens each desolate door;
And learn of the lowly and meek to lessen your thoughtless pride.

I have seen my Lady flash by—a beauteous vision of ease;
I have seen the widow at work till the shadows of night fled the day;
I have seen God's poor drink the cup of sorrow and toil to the lees;
I have seen the wicked get wealth, and the good go empty away.

"The poor are unworthy, and sinning is found in the homes of the low.
If we give we but pander to vice: the beggars our gifts will abuse."
So say you, and pass in your pride, but your heart cries out as you go,
"The vile are the first to ape virtue; the wicked the first to accuse!"

Communist? Not I! But I hold that the miser who hugs
to his heart
What for him is but clay and a curse, but to some would
be blessing and bread,
Is selling his merciful Saviour. Better throw down the price
and depart;
Better, belike, do as Judas, put a rope to his miserable head.

'Twould be well with you, Midas, to pity the poor who are
tarrying here.
They may count to your just condemnation the tears which
their hungry babes weep.
Though you harden your heart for a lifetime, and turn an
adamant ear,
Their wails may pierce through to your coffin and trouble
your long, last sleep.

How read you the Scriptures? What say they? "These three
with the world now abide,
Hope, charity, faith, and the greatest is charity—blessed
above all."
Our hands should be fruitful and open. The field for our
giving is wide,
And blessing shall follow the gifts, though the power to give
may be small.

Then time may toil on with its tumults, its troubles and
tempests of tears;
The sweet, voiceless shadows shall hold us till striving and
sorrow are past.
We shall wake full refreshed to the judgment, though we
slumber for eons of years;
And the Lord shall show us His glory, we shall be like to
God at the last.

A Dream Fulfilled

Thirsting for bounteous Nature's ease
I spread my white sail to the breeze,
And through the crystal balm of morn
My airy birch was softly borne.

A blue league to the verdant west
Sleep on the Saint John's placid breast,
Like second Edens kindly lent,
The bosky Islands of Content.

All day their beauty was my own;
And there, when deep-eyed night came down,
In rapturous dreams I viewed again
The glories of my bright domain.

I saw the dawn blow gold and red,
By fluted robins heralded;
While over meadows starred with dew
Inspiring airs of nature blew.

Like silver gleaming, white like snow,
Rose-tinted in that throbbing glow,
The blue its drifting clouds displayed,
Dappling the fields with light and shade.

The wafted mist-wreaths, melting, shed
The scent of flowers which they had fed;
And lakelets gleamed with lilies white,
And vales with buttercups grew bright.

The infinite secrets of the trees
Rustled unreadably in the breeze,
And through the brooding of my dream
Rang white-capped laughter of the stream.

I saw the grape-vine spreading o'er
The tangled thickets by the shore,
Where ferns and milk-weed, cherry spray,
And fronded sumachs cooled the day.

I heard the buzzing sea-like hush
Of wild bees in the willow bush,
And through the honeysuckle stirred
The sleep-song of the humming-bird.

The white gull soared with wings agleam,
The golden perch shone in the stream,
And on the weed-caught log the crane
Pecked at his captured shells again.

Through restful hours thus stole away
The perfect, consummated day;
And in the sky, and in the stream,
I saw the sunset's glory gleam.

And ere the golden glow passed by,
The silvery moonlight filled the sky;
Like sister angels kissing, they,
The waxing night and waning day!

Then with the setting of the sun
The circle of my dream was run,
And, half awake, the vision flown,
I felt the bondage of the town.

But recollection swiftly came:
I roused, and saw the east aflame,
And lo, before my raptured eyes
My dreams became realities!

Ethelwyn Wetherald

Many of our Confederation Poets had fathers who were clergymen, and Agnes Ethelwyn Wetherald was no exception. But in her case the Reverend William Wetherald was a Quaker, and he was the founder of the Rockwood Academy. Our poet was born on April 26, 1857 in Rockwood, Ontario, where she was educated at her father's school. She later attended the Friends' Boarding School in Union Springs, New York. Wetherald's Quaker upbringing set the foundation for her future work. Upon her return to Canada, she worked in Toronto as a proofreader and editorial assistant, but city life did not suit her.

Wetherald was chiefly a poet of nature, and her poetry of birds has never been surpassed. *The Last Robin: Lyrics and Sonnets*, her most important book, appeared in 1907. When it was published, Earl Grey, the Governor General of Canada, bought twenty-five copies to give to his friends. She was also a feminist and wrote about the ill treatment of women, as in "Hester Prynne Speaks", a poem based on Nathaniel Hawthorne's novel *The Scarlet Letter*. Unhappy with the big city, Wetherald moved to the Niagara Peninsula, where she died on March 9, 1940 at Pelham, Ontario.

April in the City

April sunshine along the street
    Is turning the motes of dust to gold.
Scant is the green to our longing feet,
    To our longing eyes few buds unfold.

    Only in vision are slopes unrolled
    And orchards full as their arms can hold,
    And stories in exquisite cadence told
By the willowed stream in its sweet retreat.

    Yet even here the heart grown cold
Flushes with sudden inward heat,
When April sunshine along the street
    Is turning the motes of dust to gold.

When It's Time for Leaves to Fly

When it's time for leaves to fly,
    Winds shall blow and leaves shall go;
When it's time for Love to die,
    Close his eyes and lay him low.

When it's time for frost to sting,
    Birds are dumb and streams are numb;
Speak not of another spring—
    Nevermore OUR spring shall come.

Nevermore our lives shall be
    What they seemed when first we dreamed,
Since the leaves of memory
    Drop where passion's river gleamed.

Youth and Age

Bent over some heroic book,
    In nights gone by, his boyish head
So filled with eager dreams he took
    Them with him to his bed.
The splendid strife, the rush of life,
    The trump of fame, inspiring, strong,
His heart so stirred he scarcely heard
    His mother's slumber song.

But now the glowing book of life
    Is falling from his nerveless hand;
Gone are the splendors of the strife,
    The conquering hopes—a daring band;
No plaudits pierce those aged ears,
    No trump of fame, though loud and strong,
He only hears across the years
    His mother's slumber song.

In Summer Rain

How vividly in summer rain
    The commonest of tints are seen;
The Robin is a scarlet stain
    Against the shining evergreen.

The last scant strawberries—a score
    That hid behind the reddening leaves—
Rain-flushed, wind-tossed, are waiting for
    Red-lipped or redder-breasted thieves.

The willows, pallid in the sun,
    Are sunny in the rainy dark,
A deeper brown the streamlets run,
    And deeply black the orchard bark.

And yet, although the clouds are gray,
  These freshening tints of every hue
Would intimate a rain at play,
  Or at the worst a storm of dew.

The quality of mercy flows
  Upon the meadow's thirsty brood,
And every brightening grass-blade shows
  The quality of gratitude.

The Sun in the Woods

The sun within the leafy woods
  Is like a midday moon,
So soft upon these solitudes
  Is bent the face of noon.

Loosed from the outside summer blaze
  A few gold arrows stray;
A vagrant brilliance droops or plays
  Through all the dusky day.

The gray trunk feels a touch of light,
  While, where dead leaves are deep,
A gleam of sunshine, golden white,
  Lies like a soul asleep.

And just beyond dank-rooted ferns,
  Where darkening hemlocks sigh
And leaves are dim, the bare road burns
  Beneath a dazzling sky.

The Song Sparrow's Nest

Here where tumultuous vines
  Shadow the porch at the west,
Leaf with tendril entwines
  Under a song sparrow's nest.

She in her pendulous nook
  Sways with the warm wind tide,
I with a pen or a book
  Rock as soft at her side.

Comrades with nothing to say,
  Neither of us intrudes,
But through the lingering day
  Each of us sits and broods.

Not upon hate and fear,
  Not upon grief or doubt,
Not upon spite or sneer,
  These we could never hatch out.

She broods on wonderful things:
  Quickening life that belongs
To a heart and a voice and wings,
  But—I'm not so sure of my songs!

Then in the summer night,
  When I awake with a start,
I think of the nest at the height—
  The leafy height of my heart;

I think of the mother love,
  Of the patient wings close furled,
Of the sky that broods above,
  Of the Love that broods on the world.

The Pasture Field

When spring has burned
　The ragged robe of winter, stitch by stitch,
And deftly turned
　To moving melody the wayside ditch,
The pale-green pasture field behind the bars
Is goldened o'er with dandelion stars.

When summer keeps
　Quick pace with sinewy, white-shirted arms,
And daily steeps
　In sunny splendor all her spreading farms,
The pasture field is flooded foamy white
With daisy faces looking at the light.

When autumn lays
　Her golden wealth upon the forest floor,
And all the days
　Look backward at the days that went before,
A pensive company the asters stand,
Their blue eyes brightening the pasture land.

When winter lifts
　A sounding trumpet to his strenuous lips,
And shapes the drifts
　To curves of transient loveliness, he slips
Upon the pasture's ineffectual brown
A swan-soft vestment delicate as down.

The Fields of Dark

The wreathing vine within the porch
  Is in the heart of me,
The roses that the noondays scorch
  Burn on in memory;
Alone at night I quench the light,
  And without star or spark
The grass and trees press to my knees,
  And flowers throng the dark.

The leaves that loose their hold at noon
  Drop on my face like rain,
And in the watches of the moon
  I feel them fall again.
By day I stray how far away
  To stream and wood and steep,
But on my track they all come back
  To haunt the vale of sleep.

The fields of light are clover-brimmed,
  Or grassed or daisy-starred;
The fields of dark are softly dimmed,
  And safely twilight-barred;
But in the gloom that fills my room
  I cannot fail to mark
The grass and trees about my knees,
  The flowers in the dark.

A Midday in Midsummer

The sky's great curtains downward steal,
  The earth's fair company
Of trees and streams and meadows feel
  A sense of privacy.

Upon the vast expanse of heat
  Light-footed breezes pace;
To waves of gold they tread the wheat,
  They lift the sunflower's face.

The cruel sun is blotted out,
  The west is black with rain,
The drooping leaves in mingled doubt
  And hope look up again.

The weeds and grass on tiptoe stand,
  A strange exultant thrill
Prepares the dazed, uncertain land
  For the wild tempest's will.

The wind grows big and breathes aloud
  As it runs hurrying past;
At one sharp blow the thunder-cloud
  Lets loose the furious blast.

The earth is beaten, drenched and drowned,
  The elements go mad;
Swift streams of joy flow o'er the ground,
  And all the leaves are glad.

Then comes a momentary lull;
  The darkest clouds are furled,
And lo, new washed and beautiful
  And breathless gleams the world!

The Prairie

Clothed in the virginal green of early spring,
Or, later, fragrant with her miles of sweet
Wild roses flushing in the summer heat,
Or mantled in a shining robe a king
Might wear when golden-rod is flowering,
Or thrilled responsive to the dancing feet
Of little laughing rains, or feeling fleet
Yet strong—how strong!—the wind's unwearied wing;

Whate'er her garb, the prairie speaks of love—
Love's virginal beginnings, rosy moods,
Her golden joys and happy, happy tears.
The mighty wing that tireless sweeps above
Her summer sweets and winter solitudes
Is weariless as love's unending years.

Youth in Age

When younger women stand a breathing space
Before their mirrors, with an inward smile
At burnished hair or slender throat or wile
Of dimpled chin, or nest a rose in lace
And note how perfectly it mates the face,
I, pallid, worn and hollow-templed, pile
My heart with thoughts of secret triumphs, while
Young hopes are mine, young bliss and youth's light pace.

For when my lover's eyes are fixed on me
There are no years, no hollows, no gray days,
No harsh realities, no endless prose;
But only flowery lanes of poetry,
Through which we wander, lost in sweet amaze
That life could hold such fairness near its close.

At Waking

When I shall go to sleep and wake again
At dawning in another world than this,
What will atone to me for all I miss?
The light melodious footsteps of the rain,
The press of leaves against my window-pane,
The sunset wistfulness and morning bliss,
The moon's enchantment, and the twilight kiss
Of winds that wander with me through the lane.

Will not my soul remember evermore
The earthly winter's hunger for the spring,
The wet sweet cheek of April, and the rush
Of roses through the summer's open door;
The feelings that the scented woodlands bring
At evening with the singing of the thrush?

The Snow-fall

The great, soft, downy snow-fall like a cloak
Descends to wrap the lean world head to feet;
It gives the dead another winding-sheet,
It buries all the roofs until the smoke
Seems like a soul that from its clay has broke;
It broods moon-like upon the autumn wheat,
And visits all the trees in their retreat,
To hood and mantle that poor shivering folk.

With wintry bloom it fills the harshest grooves
In jagged pine stump fences; every sound
It hushes to the footstep of a nun;
Sweet Charity, that brightens where it moves,
Inducing darkest bits of churlish ground
To give a radiant answer to the sun.

The Silent Snow

To-day the earth has not a word to speak.
The snow comes down as softly through the air
As pitying heaven to a martyr's prayer,
Or white grave roses to a bloodless cheek.
The footsteps of the snow, as white and meek
As angel travellers, are everywhere—
On fence and brier and up the forest stair,
And on the wind's trail o'er the moorland bleak.

They tread the rugged road as tenderly
As April venturing her first caress;
They drown the old earth's furrowed griefs and scars
Within the white foam of a soundless sea,
And bring a deeper depth of quietness
To graves asleep beneath the silent stars.

William Douw Lighthall

William Douw Lighthall was born on December 27, 1857 in Hamilton, Ontario, but his family moved to Montréal, where he studied law at McGill University. He practiced law in that city until 1944. Although a fine poet, his initial contribution to Canadian literature was an anthology he edited, *Songs of the Great Dominion: Voices from the Forests and Waters, the Settlements and Cities of Canada* (1889). Lighthall's was the first anthology to offer work by our Confederation Poets, and eleven of the sixteen poets in the present anthology—George Frederick Cameron, Wilfred Campbell, Bliss Carman, Isabella Valancy Crawford, S. Frances Harrison, E. Pauline Johnson, Archibald Lampman, Sir Charles G.D. Roberts, Duncan Campbell Scott, Frederick George Scott, and Barry Straton—appear in his *Songs*.

But he is included here as a poet, not an editor, and as a poet he followed his idea that the four founding people of Canada were the Indigenous People, the French settlers, the British settlers, and the United Empire Loyalists, who came to Canada following the American Revolution. Each group contributed something compelling to the making of Canada in 1867. And Lighthall honoured them in his own poetry. He lived into his late nineties, dying on August 3, 1954 at Montréal, Québec.

Canada Not Last

1881

At Venice

Lo! Venice, gay with color, lights and song,
Calls from St. Mark's with ancient voice and strange:
I am the Witch of Cities! glide along
My silver streets that never wear by change
Of years: forget the years, and pain, and wrong,
And every sorrow reigning men among.
Know I can soothe thee, please and marry thee
To my illusions. Old and siren-strong,
I smile immortal, while the mortals flee
Who whiten on to death in wooing me.

At Florence

What fairer is, by Arno's bridgéd gleam,
Than Florence, viewed from San Miniato's slope
At eventide, when west along the stream,
The last of day reflects a silver hope!—
Lo, all else softened in the twilight beam:—
The city's mass blent in one hazy cream,
The brown Dome midst it, and the Lily tower,
And grey Old Tower more near, and hills that seem
Afar, like clouds to fade, and hills of power
On this side, greenly dark with cypress, vine and bower.

At Rome

End of desire to stray I feel would come
Though Italy were all blue skies to me,
Though France's fields went mad with flowery foam
And Blanc put on a special majesty.
Not all could match the growing thought of home
Nor tempt to exile. Look I not on ROME—
This ancient, modern, mediæval queen—
Yet still sigh westward over hill and dome,
Imperial ruin and villa's princely scene
Lovely with pictured saints and marble gods serene.

Reflection

Rome, Florence, Venice—noble, fair and quaint,
They reign in robes of magic round me here;
But fading, blotted, dim, a picture faint,
With spell more silent, only pleads a tear.
Plead not! Thou hast my heart, O picture dim!
I see the fields, I see the autumn hand
Of God upon the maples! Answer Him
With weird, translucent glories, ye that stand
Like spirits in scarlet and in amethyst!
I see the sun break over you; the mist
On hills that lift from iron bases grand
Their heads superb!—the dream, it is my native land.

The Caughnawaga Beadwork Seller

Kanawâki—"By the Rapid,"—
Low the sunset midst thee lies;
And from the wild Reservation
Evening's breeze begins to rise.
Faint the Kônoronkwa chorus
Drifts across the current strong;
Spirit-like the parish steeple
Stands thy ancient walls among.

Kanawâki—"By the Rapid,"—
How the sun amidst thee burns!
Village of the Praying Nation,
Thy dark child to thee returns.
All day through the pale-face city,
Silent, selling beaded wares,
I have wandered with my basket,
Lone, excepting for their stares!

They are white men; we are Indians;
What a gulf their stares proclaim!
They are mounting; we are dying;
All our heritage they claim.
We are dying, dwindling, dying,
Strait and smaller grows our bound;
They are mounting up to heaven
And are pressing all around.

Thou art ours,—little remnant,
Ours through countless thousand years—
Part of the old Indian world,
Thy breath from far the Indian cheers.
Back to thee, O Kanawâki!
Let the rapids dash between
Indian homes and white men's manners—
Kanawâki and Lachine!

O my dear! O Knife-and-Arrows!
Thou art bronzed, thy limbs are lithe;
How I laugh as through the crosse-game,
Slipst thou like red elder withe.
Thou art none of these pale-faces!
When with thee I'll happy feel,
For thou art the Mohawk warrior
From thy scalp-lock to thy heel.

Sweet the Kônoronkwa chorus
Floats across the current strong;
Clear behold the parish steeple
Rise the ancient walls among.
Speed us deftly, noiseless paddle:
In my shawl my bosom burns!
Kanawâki—"By the Rapid,"—
Thine own child to thee returns.

Winter's Dawn in Lower Canada

To each there lives some beauteous sight: mine is to me most fair,
I carry fadeless one clear dawn in keen December air,
O'er leagues of plain from night we fled upon a pulsing train;
For breath of morn, outside I stood. Then up a carmine stain
Flushed calm and rich the long, low east, deep reddening till the sun
Eyed from its molten fires and shot strange arrows, one by one
On certain fields, and on a wood of distant evergreen,
And fairy opal blues and pinks on all the snows between:
(Broad earth had never such a flower as in my country grows,
When at the rising winter sun, the plain is all a rose.)
Then seemed all nymphs and gods awake—heaven brightened with their smiles,
The land was theirs; like mirages, stood out Elysian isles.
Westward the forests smiled in strength and glory like the plain,

Their bare boughs rose, an arrowy flight, and by them sped the train.
But dream-crown of that porcelain sea, those plains of sunrise snow,
The green woods east, the grey woods west, and molten carmine glow—
A light flashed through the sapling wastes and alders nearer by,
Where Phœbus worked the spell of spells that ever charmed an eye,
His bright spears to the frost-flakes reached, that on their branches lay,
And each shot back, as we sped by, a single peerless ray.
More bright than starry hosts appeared that vision in the wood
And flashed and flew like fire-flies in a nightly solitude,
A maze of silver stars, a dance of diamonds in the day:
Through many lives though fly my soul as on that pulsing train,
That sparkling dawn shall oftentimes enkindle it again.

Deathless

October 30, 1917

Each ripe maple leaf before it falls has at the base of its stalk a fully formed next year's leaf in shape of a bud.

I

In the rugged limestone pasture
The old hard maple glows,
With burning tone and glory,
Like the sun in all its sunset,
In the rich Laurentian autumn
The sunset of the year.

II

At Passchendaele I saw it
When the battlefield was fading,
And the roar of guns grew silent
When my life stream stopped its flowing,
I saw the old hard maple
And her fire of leaves embraced me
As my life fell off in glory,
In the sunset of the year.

III

The old hard maple glowing
With dying fire and splendor
Hid at her every leafstalk,
The perfect bud of spring,
At the root of the leaf of glory,
Of the dying leaf of splendor,
The leaf of morrow year.

IV

At Passchendaele I sleep not,
Only my leaves of autumn,
My autumn leaves fell there,
In the hour of farewell splendor
In the sunset of the year,
But when they fell I died not,
For the wondrous spring was in me
And the life I gave at Passchendaele
Hid the life of morrow year—
I am here.

February 3, 1918

To France

We knew thee, France, in times of peace,
    And willing sought thy gracious thrall;
The modern heir of ancient Greece,
    The kind, the gay, the light of all;

We knew thee, yet we knew thee not,
    Sun-tressed Minerva of the Dawn!
Till by thy dauntless side we fought
    Darkness and all its Satan-spawn!

Again shall peace and light return
    Again men's hearts shall flock to thee
How bright thy beacons then shall burn!
    How deep our homage then shall be!

Then thou shalt build thy noblest Arch,
    Then thou shalt sing thy song supreme,
And all the world shall join thy march
    Toward thy best and greatest dream!

May 26, 1918

Commandant's Isle

Chief Commandant was the last Indian resident at
    Lac Tremblant.

Last of your tribe and long departed hence,
Algonkin brave, here unto whom was given,
To close the chapter of primeval man.
Each night returning to your cedared isle
I see your fire upon the Sandy Point,—

The stick-supported pot, the shadowy lodge,
The deerskin soaking by the shore, the gleam
Of trout, the ghostly smoke, and round the glow,
The ruddy, blackhaired children, turned to you
Their other sun, and you recounting lore.

What ancient legends of the wilderness!
What doomsday record of old valiant chiefs!
What explanations of some pictured rock
Or carven pine! What battles in the woods,
Centuries ago, with the Bad Iroquois!
What ghostly tales of giant windigoes,—
Cunning man-eaters, black and terrible,
Long-following, undesisting,—vanquished now,—
By sign of cross, and of man-hunger dead—
Only their shrivelled bodies here and there
Descried among gaunt trunks of blackened trees.
    And then upon the glowing logs you cast
The sacred leaves, and as the incense mounts
The stories of Ewitchi you retell,
Pointing to the faint moondawn on the heights.
Full of the sense of spirit you and yours
Familiarly knew the living fays
We call the flowers, each as full of joy
As full of beauty, each with speaking voice
And hearing ear, and when its sleeptime comes
Ready to dream, and rise another spring.
To you the forests were all breathing men,
Fair women and loved children:—even the chase
A strife of cousins, preordained in rites.

You were Ewitchi's children like the rest,
Part of his ordered subjects:—all your hours
Moved with celestial dial hands, the dawn
Noon, sunset, evening, night; the birchbark frail

Of your life sailed on beauty as a lake:
Princes you were of all to be desired.

Commandant—it was almost yesterday
Your fire glowed on the Sandy Point. To-day
Your spirit only, haunts the cedared isle.
Who is the dream? Is it ourselves or you?
Dreamland you left us. Is there chance the mist
Some morn may lift and your canoe be seen—
Gumsewn, with ochre eye upon its prow—
Forth setting to your traps in Fleurant Bay?
Or might it be your earliest ancestor?
Who first, a hundred thousand years ago
Came paddling up the wide and silent Lake
Gazing in wonder at the mighty Mount.
And to Ewitchi made his sacrifice,
And cut his birchen poles and built his lodge
And lit his fire upon the Sandy Point
As you and all your fathers since have done.

Calm rest to you, Algonkin! May your lot
Be cast in scenes as lovely as this isle
That sits above its double on the Lake,
Its greatest charm these memories of you.

Homer

Early lines

Time, with his constant touch, has half erased
The memory, but he cannot dim the fame
　　Of one who best of all has paraphrased
The tale of waters with a tale of flame,
Yet left us but his accents and his name.

Upon that life, the sun of history
Shines not, but Legend, like a moon in mist,
    Sheds over it a weird uncertainty,
In which all figures wave and actions twist,
So that a man may read them as he list.

We know not if he trod some Theban street,
And sought compassion on his aged woe,
    We know not if on Chian sand his feet
Left footprints once; but only this we know,
How the high ways of fame those footprints show.

Along the border of the restless sea,
The lonely thinker must have loved to roam,
    We feel his soul wrapt in its majesty,
And he can speak in words that drip with foam,
As though himself a deep, and depths his home.

Hark! under all and through and over all,
Runs on the cadence of the changeful sea;
    Now pleasantly the graceful surges fall,
And now they mutter in an angry key
Ever, throughout their changes, strong and free.

How sternly sang he of Achilles' might,
How sweetly of the sweet Andromache,
    How low his lyre when Ajax prays for light;
(Well might he bend that lyre in sympathy,
For also great, and also blind was he.)

We almost see the nod of sternbrowed Jove,
And feel Olympus shake; we almost hear
    The melodies that Greek youths interwove
In pæan to Apollo, and the clear,
Full voice of Nestor, sounding far and near.

S. Frances Harrison

Susan Frances Harrison, who commonly used the *nom de plume* Seranus, was born on February 24, 1859 in Toronto, Ontario. She would die at age seventy-six in the city of her birth on May 5, 1935. Despite being a Torontonian, having studied for a couple of years in Montréal, Harrison developed a life-long love of Québec and of Québécois culture. Her Montréal experiences had a lasting effect on her poetry. This is indicated by the title of her debut poetry collection, *Pine, Rose and Fleur de Lis* (1891).

Harrison also maintained an impressive journalistic career, writing for *The Globe* (forerunner of *The Globe and Mail*), the (Detroit) *Free Press*, and writing for and briefly editing *The Week*. In this way our poet became a public intellectual. But she is presented here as a poet, and as a poet she favoured the sonnet and, especially, the villanelle. In addition to her six volumes of poetry and her fiction, Harrison composed music such as her "String Quartet on Ancient Irish Airs" and piano versions of traditional Québécois airs. She was an influential cultural figure of her day.

Nocturne

O Summer on the lake is fair,
Yet chilly when the sun has fled,
Yet damp where clings the cool night air!

Wrapped in our cloaks we sit just where
We'll watch the moon her measure tread,
O Summer on the lake is fair!

In town the people in despair
Bewail the heat in torment dread.
Though damp where clings the cool night air,

We do not fear its breath to share,
Nor dream of such a thing as bed—
O Summer on the lake is fair!

The breeze it blows about the hair,
The boat is warm with wraps o'erspread,
Yet damp where clings the cool night air;

To Heaven there winds a starry stair,
A diamond world is overhead—
O Summer on the lake is fair,
Yet damp where clings the cool night air!

At St. Hilaire

Combien des enfans? Why, twenty-five!
Now, by all the Gods and every Saint,
I wonder the woman is left alive

To tell the tale! How many survive?
    She answers me, calm and without constraint,
"Combien? Mossieu? Why, twenty-five."

Not *one* ever lost? Not one; they thrive,
    Do little ones in this parish quaint.
I wonder the woman is left alive,

Who has less than twelve. The bigger the hive,
    The greater the honour, no sign of complaint—
Combien des enfans? Why, twenty-five.

The men don't care and the priests contrive
    At mass the duty of parents to paint,
But I wonder the women are left alive.

Here come Antoine, Josephte, Max, who drive
    The rest—fifteen. At the sight you faint.
Combien des enfans? Why, twenty-five!
I wonder the woman is left alive.

Tintern Abbey

To wear its image—seal'd—fix'd mentally,
Pinn'd to my heart's eyes—old, smooth-worn, gray stone,
Green-lichen'd, ivy-curtain'd, blossom-blown
In stray sweet crevices—this is fealty!
O, I could never look enough, but see
Some new divinity each second, grown
By the potent centuries—guardians. There, alone,
Girdled by hills it rested, and to me
The great rose window form'd a glorious fane,
Mightier than other I had ever seen,
And when I lifted awed eyes, finite brain

To the open blue, where once a roof had been,
I knew from innumerable, awful winnowings—
There was more room for our great God's wide wings.

November

These are the days that try us; these the hours
That find, or leave us, cowards—doubters of Heaven,
Sceptics of self, and riddled through with vain
Blind questionings as to Deity. Mute, we scan
The sky, the barren, wan, the drab, dull sky,
And mark it utterly blank. Whereas, a fool,
The flippant fungoid growth of modern mode,
Uncapped, unbelled, unshorn, but still a fool,
Fate at his fingers' ends, and Cause in tow,
Or, wiser, say, the Yorick of his age,
The Touchstone of his period, would forecast
Better than us, the film and foam of rose
That yet may float upon the eastern grays
At dawn to-morrow.
Still, and if we could,
We would not change our gloom for glibness, lose
Our wonder in our faith. We are not worse
Than those in whom the myth was strongest, those
In whom first awe lived longest, those who found
—Dear Pagans—gods in fountain, flood and flower.
Sometimes the old Hellenic base stirs, live,
Within us, and we thrill to branch and beam
When walking where the aureoled autumn sun
Looms golden through the chestnuts. But to-day—
When sodden leaves are merged in melting mire,
And garden-plots lie pilfered, and the vines
Are strings of tangled rigging reft of green,
Crude harps whereon the winter wind shall play

His bitter music—on a day like this,
We, harbouring no Hellenic images, stand
In apathy mute before our window pane,
And muse upon the blankness. Then, O, then,
If ever, should we thank our God for those
Rare spirits who have testified in faith
Of such a world as this, and straight we pray
For such an eye as Wordsworth's, he who saw
System in anarchy, progress in ruin, peace
In devastation. Duty was his star—
May it be ours—this Star the Preacher missed.

The Tree

Was there no beauty, then, in barren stem,
  No symmetry in jagged twig and limb,
That slow discarding lustrous diadem
  Lay etched upon the sunset's orange rim?

Were it, too, better never to have been
  A thing leaf-crowned and wholly, freshly fair;
A being all benignant, purely green,
  Sheltered and sheltering, innocent of care?

Strange—that for half the year the tree must go
  Uncrowned, unclad, soul-shivering to the blast,
Each glossy leaf be trodden deep in snow,
  Each acorn to the ground be roughly cast!

Careless of coming frost aloft it looks,
  All confident of many another spring,
O'er dry, brown fields and saddened, silent brooks,
  And woods where not a bird is left to sing.

This the great secret of its grand content,
  This the full meaning of its giant calm,
This the true measure of the reverent
  Straight mien that springtime's sweetest airs embalm.

O, to have been the tree—and not the man!
  To grow in ever wheeling, circling pride,
Conscious of all the noble, gracious plan
  That smiled at Doubt and gave a God to guide!

Think! to have harboured orange oriole,
  And flaming tanager and chattering jay,
And wise gray sparrow—would not this console
  The weariness born of many a leafless day?

Since it were known—they come again in five
  Or six months' time of waiting, then to wait,
Even through songless seasons, were to thrive
  On sweet probation, though in sombre state.

Were it not bliss, some melting morn in June,
  To look and see among one's crumpled leaves—
Late to unfold, but deep at heart in tune
  With all of green the young wood interweaves—

A flash of living light, incarnate gem,
  That holds a voice in quivering, ruffled throat,
That hangs, a jewel, on the budding stem,
  That sings a song of Hope—Death's antidote?

In March

Here on the wide waste lands,
Take—child—these trembling hands,
Though my life be as blank and waste,
My days as surely ungraced
By glimmer of green on the rim
Of a sunless wilderness dim,
As the wet fields barren and brown,
As the fork of each sterile limb
Shorn of its lustrous crown.

See—how vacant and flat
The landscape—empty and dull,
Scared by an ominous lull
Into a trance—we have sat
This hour on the edge of a broken, a gray snake-fence,
And nothing that lives has flown,
Or crept, or leapt, or been blown
To our feet or past our faces—
So desolate, child—the place is!
It strikes, does it not, a chill,
Like that other upon the hill,
We felt one bleak October?
See—the gray wood still sober
'Ere it be wild with glee,
With growth, with an ecstasy
Of fruition born of desire.
The marigold's yellow fire
Doth not yet in the sun burn to leap, to aspire;
Its myriad spotted spears
No erythronium rears;
We cannot see
Anemone,
Or heart-lobed brown hepatica;

There doth not fly,
Low under sky,
One kingfisher—dipping and darting
From reedy shallows where reds are starting,
Pale pink tips that shall burst into bloom,
Not in one night's mid-April gloom,
But inch by inch, till ripening tint,
And feathery plume and emerald glint
Proclaim the waters are open.

All this will come,
The panting hum
Of the life that will stir,
Glance and glide, and whistle and whir,
Chatter and crow, and perch and pry,
Crawl and leap and dart and fly,
Things of feather and things of fur,
Under the blue of an April sky.
Shall speak, the dumb,
Shall leap, the numb,
All this will come,
It never misses,
Failure, yet—
Never was set
In the sure spring's calendar,
Wherefore—Pet—
Give me one of your springtime kisses!
While you plant some hope in my cold man's breast—
Ah! How welcome the strange flower-guest—
Water it softly with maiden tears,
Go to it early—and late—with fears;
Guard it, and watch it, and give it time
For the holy dews to moisten the rime—
Make of it some green gracious thing,
Such as the Heavens shall make of the Spring!

The Marshes

In mist-draped pools, lagoons of dull dark green,
A league along the broad lakeshore they wind.
Gray skies at morn and blue at noon but find
And leave them dim and dank, the fit demesne
Of writhing things and creeping, dismal grave
Of crimes unknown, where knotted ends of rope
Twist, tangle around the slimy roots that grope
For fresher air unwashed by a fetid wave.

Yet out upon these marshes there is glow,
Radiance illimitable, when the crest
Of distant hills is outlined black below
The broken splendours of the burning West.
Then, each tall rush becomes an argent spire,
Then, the dim pools are flooded red with fire.

At Valois

Long leafy headlands stretch into the green
Of mighty Saint Laurent, while on the mead,
Dark Ottawa's tawny waters rush and recede;
Dorval floats, shimmering; turbulent Lachine
Sparkles in dipping silver crests between
Rich shores of elm, fringed with glistering reed;
That dim red web is the bridge; around us speed
The brown canoes, for sunset port grown keen.

Ah! It is summer sweet; it is fair, it is fair!
That tapering spire to the right is little Pointe Claire.
Afar in the sun-flushed fields a woman stands
Motionless, resting, behind her antique plough,
Shading from too much glare a beautiful brow
With sunburnt, resolute, hard and horny hands.

Wilfred Campbell

Although there is some doubt as to the date and place of William Wilfred Campbell's birth, it seems most likely that the poet was born on June 15, 1860 in Newmarket, Ontario. More importantly, he graduated from secondary school in Owen Sound at the foot of the Bruce Peninsula on Georgian Bay. This led him to become the Poet of the Lake Region, as he called that area of the Great Lakes. Campbell clearly saw our Great Lakes as a Canadian version of Wordsworth's English Lake District, although on a *much* larger scale.

Campbell wrote many volumes of poetry, perhaps his finest being *Lake Lyrics and Other Poems* (1889). In addition, he edited *The Oxford Book of Canadian Verse* in 1913, which established the importance of the Confederation Poets. He eventually moved to Ottawa, where he wrote, with fellow Confederation Poets Archibald Lampman and Duncan Campbell Scott, "At The Mermaid Inn" for Toronto's *Globe* newspaper (1892–1893). Because the topics covered in their column were wide-ranging and dealt with much of the social and cultural life of the nation, these poets influenced society as a whole. Campbell served as a drill sergeant of the Home Guard during the First World War. He died of pneumonia on January 1, 1918 at Ottawa, Ontario.

Indian Summer

Along the line of smoky hills
The crimson forest stands,
And all the day the blue-jay calls
Throughout the autumn lands.

Now by the brook the maple leans
With all his glory spread,
And all the sumachs on the hills
Have turned their green to red.

Now by great marshes wrapt in mist,
Or past some river's mouth,
Throughout the long, still autumn day
Wild birds are flying south.

On Christmas Eve

In byre and barn the mows are brim with sheaves,
Where stealeth in with phosphorescent tread
The glimmering moon, and, 'neath his wattled eaves,
The kennelled hound unto the darkness grieves
His chilly straw, and from his gloom-lit shed,
The wakeful cock proclaims the midnight dread.

With mullioned windows, 'mid its skeleton trees,
Beneath the moon the ancient manor stands;
Old gables rattle in the midnight breeze,
Old elms make answer to the moaning seas
Beyond the moorlands, on the wintry sands,
While drives the gust along the leafless lands.

Vapor and Blue

Domed with the azure of heaven,
Floored with a pavement of pearl,
Clothed all about with a brightness
Soft as the eyes of a girl,

Girt with a magical girdle,
Rimmed with a vapor of rest—
These are the inland waters,
These are the lakes of the west.

Voices of slumberous music,
Spirits of mist and of flame,
Moonlit memories left here
By gods who long ago came,

And vanishing left but an echo
In silence of moon-dim caves,
Where haze-wrapt the August night slumbers,
Or the wild heart of October raves.

Here where the jewels of nature
Are set in the light of God's smile,
Far from the world's wild throbbing,
I will stay me and rest me awhile.

And store in my heart old music,
Melodies gathered and sung
By the genies of love and of beauty
When the heart of the world was young.

To the Lakes

Blue, limpid, mighty, restless lakes,
God's mirrors underneath the sky,
Low rimmed in woods and mists, where wakes,
Through murk and moon, the marsh bird's cry.

Where ever on, through drive and drift,
'Neath blue and grey, through hush and moan,
Your ceaseless waters ebb and lift
Past shores of century-crumbling stone.

And under ever-changing skies,
Swell, throb, and break on kindling beach;
Where fires of dawn responsive rise,
In answer to your mystic speech.

Past lonely haunts of gull and loon,
Past solitude of land-locked bays,
Whose bosoms rise to meet the moon,
Beneath their silvered film of haze.

Where mists and fogs in ghostly bands,
Vague, dim, moon-clothed in spectral light;
Drift in from far-off haunted lands,
Across the silences of night.

Sunset, Lake Huron

September

The sunbeams fall in golden flakes,
    Like snow-banks flamed the clouds are furled;
The soft light shakes
On wave that breaks
    On wave, far round the gleaming world.

Great brown, bare rocks, wet, purple dyed,
    By sunsets' beams, hedge in this realm
Of sky and wide,
Bleak sweep of tide,
    Grey, tossed, scarce-plowed by keel or helm.

The east looms dark, the red day dips
    Down under gleaming rock and wave,
In hushed eclipse,
While grey night slips
    The cerements of her shrouded grave.

And buildeth up her arches dark,
    From ruins of the dim dead day,
Till earth may mark
Each luminous spark,
    Of stars that far in heaven stray.

And weaveth with her phantom hands
    (Blind, dumb, save for the moon's white wreath,
And rude wind bands
From Eblis lands)
    A shroud for the great lake beneath;

That beats and moans, a prisoned thing,
    Rock-manacled beneath the night;
And tells each shore,
Forever more
    Its sorrow in the pallid light.

The Tides of Dawn

How cool across the lake's pearled, heaving floor,
    The spirit winds of morning steal in here:
    Dim mists of darkness rise from marsh and mere,
And pallid phantoms brood at morning's door.
Beyond yon east the surfs of dawning roar,
    To break in flame-waves on night's sombre beach;
    The heart still hears their impetuous, golden speech,
Imploring morn the daylight to restore.

Soon, soon, across the night's gray, ruined walls,
    Will flood and surge the crimson tides of morn;
    Bathing the east and all the dusks forlorn;
Soon, soon, across the dawn's white silence falls
    Glory and music, morning's song and fire:
    The waking world leaps to the day's desire.

Medwayosh

A world of dawn, where sky and water merge
    In far, dim vapors, mingling blue in blue,
    Where low-rimmed shores shimmer like gold shot through
Some misty fabric. Lost in dreams, I urge
With languid oar my skiff through sunny surge,
    That rings its music round the rocks and sands,
    Passing to silence, where far lying lands
Loom blue and purpling from the morning's verge.

I linger in dreams, and through my dreaming comes,
Like sound of suffering heard through battle drums,
An anguished call of sad, heart-broken speech;
As if some wild lake spirit, long ago
Soul-wronged, through hundred years its wounded woe
Moans out in vain across each wasted beach.

Alone

Here in the night I sit alone,
Where far above the aged roof,
Half mossed, and half with vines o'er-grown,
The starlight weaves a silver woof,
And falls in flakes where all unknown,
Out in the night I sit alone.

Here all alone where only comes
The moon's white feet before the dawn,
I sit and list the dreary hums
Of night sounds where all life is gone,
While night its lonely cycle sums,
And wait a *step* that never comes.

'Tis only for a ghost I wait,
The wraith of something gone before,
Some past, some sweet, long-dreamed-of state,
Whose memory is my only store;
Like Lazarus at the rich man's gate,
Here 'neath the stars I watch and wait.

I watch and wait, but never comes
The voice I long had loved to hear,
Through weary hours the cricket hums
Weird music, and the night is drear,
And while its lonely cycle sums,
I wait a step that never comes.

Infancy

Weak, helpless wanderer from an unknown shore,
  Frail infant bark, but lately set adrift
  On life's rough waves, beneath its angry lift.
To dare its strife, and meet its tempest roar,
Thy very weakness were thy richest store.
  Thou puny tyrant, love's own gladdest gift,
  Thou blossom fallen down the world's blue rift,
How thou dost coil about the heart's deep core.

O crowing lips and dimpled, clinging hands,
  Clear, laughing eyes and chubby, baby face,
  This world without thee were an empty place.
Thou makest paradise of all earth's lands,
  And bring'st a boon no other joys can grant,
  Thou latest bond in love's sweet covenant.

On a Summer Shore

Long years have gone, and yet it seems
  But scarce an hour ago,
I lay upon a moss-grown rock,
  And watched the ebb and flow
Of waters, where cool shades above
  Glassed in cool depths below.

You stood beside me sweet and fair,
  A basket on your arm,
Red-heaped with luscious fruit we'd picked
  Down at the old shore-farm;
You stood and in the shore-wood made
  A picture glad and warm.

Like heaving pearl the blue bay rocked
  Against its limestone wall,
Far off in reeling dreams of blue
  The heavens seemed to fall
About the world, and there you stood,
  Unconscious, queen of all.

From far-off fields the low of kine,
  Soft bird-notes, airy streams,
That stole in here, far, broken notes
  Of all the day's hushed dreams;
And you, one slender shaft of light,
  In all the world's wide gleams.

We spoke no love, for I was shy,
  And you were shyer then;
Mine was a boy's faint heart, and yours
  Still outside of love's ken;
But such sweet moments are full rare
  In barren years of men.

And often when the heart is worn
  And life grows sorrow-wise,
I dream again a blue, north bay,
  A gleam of summer skies;
And by my side a young girl stands
  With heaven in her eyes.

You are a dream, a face, a wraith,
  You drift across my pain,
I lock you in my sacred past
  Where all love's ghosts remain;
But life hath nought for me so sweet
  As you can bring again.

In the Spring Fields

There dwells a spirit in the budding year—
As motherhood doth beautify the face—
That even lends these barren glebes a grace,
And fills grey hours with beauty that were drear
And bleak when the loud, storming March was here:
A glamor that the thrilled heart dimly traces
In swelling boughs and soft, wet, windy spaces,
And sunlands where the chattering birds make cheer.

I thread the uplands where the wind's footfalls
Stir leaves in gusty hollows, autumn's urns.
Seaward the river's shining breast expands,
High in the windy pines a lone crow calls,
And far below some patient ploughman turns
His great black furrow over steaming lands.

Glory of the Dying Day

O glory of the dying day!
That into darkness fades away.
O violet splendor! melting down
By river bend o'er tower and town;
O glory of the dying day!
That into darkness fades away.

O majesty of dying light!
O splendor of the gates of night!
That all a molten glory glows,
Till purple-crimson fades to rose,
And dying, melting, outward goes
In ashes on the even's rim
When all the world grows faint and dim.

O silvern sound of far-off bells!
  Ringing, ringing miles away,
Over river fields and fells,
  Round the crimson and the grey:
Pealing softly evening out
  As the dewy dusk comes down,
And the great night folds about
  River, woodlands, hills, and town.

O glory of the fading hills,
  Splendor of the river's breast,
O silence that the whole world fills,
  Sanctity of peaceful rest!
Alien from the care of day,
  Now a petalled star peeps in,
  Now night's choruses begin,
Musical and far away.

O glory of the dying day,
When my life's evening fades away,
May it in splendid peace go down
Like yours o'er river-bend and town;
Not into silence blind and stark,
Not into wintry muffled dark,
  But heralded by stars divine,
May my life's latest evening ray
  Melt into such a night as thine.

September in the Laurentian Hills

Already Winter in his sombre round,
  Before his time, hath touched these hills austere
With lonely flame. Last night, without a sound,
  The ghostly frost walked out by wood and mere.

And now the sumach curls his frond of fire,
The aspen-tree reluctant drops his gold,
And down the gullies the North's wild vibrant lyre
Rouses the bitter armies of the cold.

O'er this short afternoon the night draws down,
With ominous chill, across these regions bleak;
Wind-beaten gold, the sunset fades around
The purple loneliness of crag and peak,
Leaving the world an iron house wherein
Nor love nor life nor hope hath ever been.

How One Winter Came in the Lake Region

For weeks and weeks the autumn world stood still,
Clothed in the shadow of a smoky haze;
The fields were dead, the wind had lost its will,
And all the lands were hushed by wood and hill,
In those grey, withered days.

Behind a mist the blear sun rose and set,
At night the moon would nestle in a cloud;
The fisherman, a ghost, did cast his net;
The lake its shores forgot to chafe and fret,
And hushed its caverns loud.

Far in the smoky woods the birds were mute,
Save that from blackened tree a jay would scream,
Or far in swamps the lizard's lonesome lute
Would pipe in thirst, or by some gnarlèd root
The tree-toad trilled his dream.

From day to day still hushed the season's mood,
The streams stayed in their runnels shrunk and dry;
Suns rose aghast by wave and shore and wood,

And all the world, with ominous silence, stood
In weird expectancy:

When one strange night the sun like blood went down,
Flooding the heavens in a ruddy hue;
Red grew the lake, the sere fields parched and brown,
Red grew the marshes where the creeks stole down,
But never a wind-breath blew.

That night I felt the winter in my veins,
A joyous tremor of the icy glow;
And woke to hear the north's wild vibrant strains,
While far and wide, by withered woods and plains,
Fast fell the driving snow.

Cape Eternity

A Giant Promontory on the Saguenay River, Quebec

About thy head where dawning wakes and dies,
Sublimity, betwixt thine awful rifts,—
'Mid mists and gloom and shattered light, uplifts
Hiding in height the measure of the skies.
Here pallid Awe forever lifts her eyes,
Through veiling haze across thy rugged clefts,
Where far and faint the sombre sunlight sifts,
'Mid loneliness and doom and dread surmise.

Here nature to this ancient silence froze,
When from the deeps thy mighty shoulders rose,
And hid the sun and moon and starry light;—
Where based in shadow of thy sunless floods,
And iron bastions, vast, forever broods,
Winter, eternal stillness, death and night.

Death

When He who built this magic wizardry
Of sky and earth and sea and human heart,
And planning brain and all that holdeth part
In fleeting joy and quick mortality,
From azure peak to purpled rim of sea,
Shall come again, and by His wizard art
Dissolve the pearl, and bid the guest depart
From this high house of being's majesty:—

May He not come as summons shrill at morn,
Or sudden tempest shaking life's frail tower,
Or angry black when storms and tempests lower;
But soft at even ere the stars be born,
And love lets down her gradual veils of sleep,
So my soul pass from splendid deep to deep.

Sir Charles G.D. Roberts

The "Father of Canadian Literature," as he is widely known, Charles George Douglas Roberts, KCMG, was born on January 10, 1860 in Douglas, New Brunswick. He was the middle of three cousins, the others being Barry Straton and Bliss Carman, to write of the Tantramar Marshes of the Bay of Fundy, and his "Tantramar Revisited" is one of the finest poems on that topic. Roberts wrote several volumes of poetry and a much greater amount of fiction. His best poems are to be found in *Songs of the Common Day and Ave!: An Ode for the Shelley Centenary* (1893), although all of his collections contain good poetry.

Roberts would often write of the piece of New Brunswick where he grew up, even after he left Canada in 1897 for New York City. He did not return to Canada until 1925. During those years abroad the poet served in the First World War as a Major, and lived a Bohemian life in the United States, England, Germany, and France. Back in Canada, Roberts served as President of the Canadian Authors Association, and he used his status to help other writers. He was knighted in 1935 by King George V. Roberts died on November 26, 1943 at Toronto, Ontario.

Mist

Its hand compassionate guards our restless sight
  Against how many a harshness, many an ill!
  Tender as sleep, its shadowy palms distil
Strange vapours that ensnare our eyes with light.
Rash eyes, kept ignorant in their own despite,
  It lets not see the unsightliness they will,
  But paints each scanty fairness fairer still,
And still deludes us to our own delight.

It fades, regathers, never quite dissolves.
  And ah that life, ah that the heart and brain
  Might keep their mist and glamour, not to know
So soon the disenchantment and the pain!
  But one by one our dear illusions go,
  Stript and cast forth as time's slow wheel revolves.

Tantramar Revisited

Summers and summers have come, and gone with the flight
  of the swallow;
Sunshine and thunder have been, storm, and winter, and frost;
Many and many a sorrow has all but died from remembrance,
Many a dream of joy fall'n in the shadow of pain.
Hands of chance and change have marred, or moulded,
  or broken,
Busy with spirit or flesh, all I most have adored;
Even the bosom of Earth is strewn with heavier shadows,—
Only in these green hills, aslant to the sea, no change!
Here where the road that has climbed from the inland valleys
  and woodlands,
Dips from the hill-tops down, straight to the base of the hills,—
Here, from my vantage-ground, I can see the scattering houses,

Stained with time, set warm in orchards, meadows, and wheat,
Dotting the broad bright slopes outspread to southward and
eastward,
Wind-swept all day long, blown by the south-east wind.
Skirting the sunbright uplands stretches a riband of meadow,
Shorn of the labouring grass, bulwarked well from the sea,
Fenced on its seaward border with long clay dykes from the turbid
Surge and flow of the tides vexing the Westmoreland shores.
Yonder, toward the left, lie broad the Westmoreland marshes,—
Miles on miles they extend, level, and grassy, and dim,
Clear from the long red sweep of flats to the sky in the distance,
Save for the outlying heights, green-rampired Cumberland Point;
Miles on miles outrolled, and the river-channels divide them,—
Miles on miles of green, barred by the hurtling gusts.

Miles on miles beyond the tawny bay is Minudie.
There are the low blue hills; villages gleam at their feet.
Nearer a white sail shines across the water, and nearer
Still are the slim, grey masts of fishing boats dry on the flats.
Ah, how well I remember those wide red flats, above tide-mark
Pale with scurf of the salt, seamed and baked in the sun!
Well I remember the piles of blocks and ropes, and the
net-reels
Wound with the beaded nets, dripping and dark from the sea!
Now at this season the nets are unwound; they hang from
the rafters
Over the fresh-stowed hay in upland barns, and the wind
Blows all day through the chinks, with the streaks of sunlight,
and sways them
Softly at will; or they lie heaped in the gloom of a loft.

Now at this season the reels are empty and idle; I see them
Over the lines of the dykes, over the gossiping grass.
Now at this season they swing in the long strong wind, thro'
the lonesome

Golden afternoon, shunned by the foraging gulls.
Near about sunset the crane will journey homeward above them;
Round them, under the moon, all the calm night long,
Winnowing soft grey wings of marsh-owls wander and wander,
Now to the broad, lit marsh, now to the dusk of the dyke.
Soon, thro' their dew-wet frames, in the live keen freshness of morning,
Out of the teeth of the dawn blows back the awakening wind.
Then, as the blue day mounts, and the low-shot shafts of the sunlight
Glance from the tide to the shore, gossamers jewelled with dew
Sparkle and wave, where late sea-spoiling fathoms of drift-net
Myriad-meshed, uploomed sombrely over the land.

Well I remember it all. The salt, raw scent of the margin;
While, with men at the windlass, groaned each reel, and the net,
Surging in ponderous lengths, uprose and coiled in its station;
Then each man to his home,—well I remember it all!

Yet, as I sit and watch, this present peace of the landscape,—
Stranded boats, these reels empty and idle, the hush,
One grey hawk slow-wheeling above yon cluster of haystacks,—
More than the old-time stir this stillness welcomes me home.
Ah, the old-time stir, how once it stung me with rapture,—
Old-time sweetness, the winds freighted with honey and salt!
Yet will I stay my steps and not go down to the marshland,—
Muse and recall far off, rather remember than see,—
Lest on too close sight I miss the darling illusion,
Spy at their task even here the hands of chance and change.

The Potato Harvest

A high bare field, brown from the plough, and borne
   Aslant from sunset; amber wastes of sky
   Washing the ridge; a clamour of crows that fly
In from the wide flats where the spent tides mourn
To yon their rocking roosts in pines wind-torn;
   A line of grey snake-fence, that zigzags by
   A pond, and cattle; from the homestead nigh
The long deep summonings of the supper horn.

Black on the ridge, against that lonely flush,
   A cart, and stoop-necked oxen; ranged beside
   Some barrels; and the day-worn harvest-folk,
Here emptying their baskets, jar the hush
   With hollow thunders. Down the dusk hillside
   Lumbers the wain; and day fades out like smoke.

Tides

Through the still dusk how sighs the ebb-tide out,
   Reluctant for the reed-beds! Down the sands
   It washes. Hark! Beyond the wan grey strand's
Low limits how the winding channels grieve,
Aware the evasive waters soon will leave
   Them void amid the waste of desolate lands,
   Where shadowless to the sky the marsh expands,
And the noon-heats must scar them, and the drought.

Yet soon for them the solacing tide returns
   To quench their thirst of longing. Ah, not so
   Works the stern law our tides of life obey!
Ebbing in the night-watches swift away,
   Scarce known ere fled forever is the flow;
   And in parched channel still the shrunk stream mourns.

When Milking-Time is Done

When milking-time is done, and over all
   This quiet Canadian inland forest home
   And wide rough pasture-lots the shadows come,
And dews, with peace and twilight voices, fall,
From moss-cooled watering-trough to foddered stall
   The tired plough-horses turn,—the barnyard loam
   Soft to their feet,—and in the sky's pale dome
Like resonant chords the swooping night-jars call.

The frogs, cool-fluting ministers of dream,
   Make shrill the slow brook's borders; pasture bars
   Down clatter, and the cattle wander through,—
Vague shapes amid the thickets; gleam by gleam
   Above the wet grey wilds emerge the stars,
   And through the dusk the farmstead fades from view.

The Salt Flats

Here clove the keels of centuries ago
   Where now unvisited the flats lie bare.
   Here seethed the sweep of journeying waters, where
No more the tumbling floods of Fundy flow,
And only in the samphire pipes creep slow
   The salty currents of the sap. The air
   Hums desolately with wings that seaward fare,
Over the lonely reaches beating low.

The wastes of hard and meagre weeds are thronged
With murmurs of a past that time has wronged;
   And ghosts of many an ancient memory
Dwell by the brackish pools and ditches blind,
In these low-lying pastures of the wind,
   These marshes pale and meadows by the sea.

The Pea-Fields

These are the fields of light, and laughing air,
   And yellow butterflies, and foraging bees,
   And whitish, wayward blossoms winged as these,
And pale green tangles like a seamaid's hair.
Pale, pale the blue, but pure beyond compare,
   And pale the sparkle of the far-off seas,
   A-shimmer like these fluttering slopes of peas,
And pale the open landscape everywhere.

From fence to fence a perfumed breath exhales
   O'er the bright pallor of the well-loved fields,—
My fields of Tantramar in summer-time;
   And, scorning the poor feed their pasture yields,
Up from the bushy lots the cattle climb,
   To graze with longing through the grey, mossed rails.

The Mowing

This is the voice of high midsummer's heat.
   The rasping vibrant clamour soars and shrills
   O'er all the meadowy range of shadeless hills,
As if a host of giant cicadæ beat
The cymbals of their wings with tireless feet,
   Or brazen grasshoppers with triumphing note
   From the long swath proclaimed the fate that smote
The clover and timothy-tops and meadowsweet.

The crying knives glide on; the green swath lies.
   And all noon long the sun, with chemic ray,
   Seals up each cordial essence in its cell,
That in the dusky stalls, some winter's day,
   The spirit of June, here prisoned by his spell,
   May cheer the herds with pasture memories.

The Clearing

Stumps, and harsh rocks, and prostrate trunks all charred,
And gnarled roots naked to the sun and rain,—
They seem in their grim stillness to complain,
And by their plaint the evening peace is jarred.
These ragged acres fire and the axe have scarred,
And many summers not assuaged their pain.
In vain the pink and saffron light, in vain
The pale dew on the hillocks stripped and marred!

But here and there the waste is touched with cheer
Where spreads the fire-weed like a crimson flood
And venturous plumes of goldenrod appear;
And round the blackened fence the great boughs lean
With comfort; and across the solitude
The hermit's holy transport peals serene.

Buckwheat

This smell of home and honey on the breeze,
This shimmer of sunshine woven in white and pink
That comes a dream from memory's visioned brink,
Sweet, sweet and strange across the ancient trees,—
It is the buckwheat, boon of the later bees,
Its breadths of heavy-headed bloom appearing
Amid the blackened stumps of this high clearing,
Freighted with cheer of comforting auguries.

But when the blunt, brown grain and red-ripe sheaves,
Brimming the low log barn beyond the eaves,
Crisped by the first frost, feel the thresher's flail,
Then flock the blue wild-pigeons in shy haste
All silently down Autumn's amber trail,
To glean at dawn the chill and whitening waste.

In September

This windy, bright September afternoon
My heart is wide awake, yet full of dreams.
The air, alive with hushed confusion, teems
With scent of grain-fields, and a mystic rune,
Foreboding of the fall of Summer soon,
Keeps swelling and subsiding; till there seems
O'er all the world of valleys, hills, and streams,
Only the wind's inexplicable tune.

My heart is full of dreams, yet wide awake.
I lie and watch the topmost tossing boughs
Of tall elms, pale against the vaulted blue;
But even now some yellowing branches shake,
Some hue of death the living green endows:—
If beauty flies, fain would I vanish too.

The Oat-Threshing

A little brown old homestead, bowered in trees
That o'er the autumn landscape shine afar,
Burning with amber and with cinnabar.
A yellow hillside washed in airy seas
Of azure, where the swallow drops and flees.
Midway the slope, clear in the beaming day,
A barn by many seasons beaten grey,
Big with the gain of prospering husbandries.

In billows round the wide red welcoming doors
High piles the golden straw; while from within,
Where plods the team amid the chaffy din,
The loud pulsation of the thresher soars,
Persistent as if earth could not let cease
This happy proclamation of her peace.

In an Old Barn

Tons upon tons the brown-green fragrant hay
O'erbrims the mows beyond the time-warped eaves,
Up to the rafters where the spider weaves,
Though few flies wander his secluded way.
Through a high chink one lonely golden ray,
Wherein the dust is dancing, slants unstirred.
In the dry hush some rustlings light are heard,
Of winter-hidden mice at furtive play.

Far down, the cattle in their shadowed stalls,
Nose-deep in clover fodder's meadowy scent,
Forget the snows that whelm their pasture streams,
The frost that bites the world beyond their walls.
Warm housed, they dream of summer, well content
In day-long contemplation of their dreams.

The Flight of the Geese

I hear the low wind wash the softening snow,
The low tide loiter down the shore. The night,
Full filled with April forecast, hath no light.
The salt wave on the sedge-flat pulses slow.
Through the hid furrows lisp in murmurous flow
The thaw's shy ministers; and hark! The height
Of heaven grows weird and loud with unseen flight
Of strong hosts prophesying as they go!

High through the drenched and hollow night their wings
Beat northward hard on winter's trail. The sound
Of their confused and solemn voices, borne
Athwart the dark to their long Arctic morn,
Comes with a sanction and an awe profound,
A boding of unknown, foreshadowed things.

Blomidon

This is that black rock bastion, based in surge,
Pregnant with agate and with amethyst,
Whose foot the tides of storied Minas scourge,
Whose top austere withdraws into its mist.
This is that ancient cape of tears and storm,
Whose towering front inviolable frowns
O'er vales Evangeline and love keep warm—
Whose fame thy song, O tender singer, crowns.
Yonder, across these reeling fields of foam,
Came the sad threat of the avenging ships.
What profit now to know if just the doom,
Though harsh! The streaming eyes, the praying lips,
The shadow of inextinguishable pain,
The poet's deathless music—these remain!

My Trees

At evening, when the winds are still,
And wide the yellowing landscape glows,
My firwoods on the lonely hill
Are crowned with sun and loud with crows.
Their flocks throng down the open sky
From far salt flats and sedgy seas;
Then dusk and dewfall quench the cry,—
So calm a home is in my trees.

At morning, when the young wind swings
The green slim tops and branches high,
Out puffs a noisy whirl of wings,
Dispersing up the empty sky.
In this dear refuge no roof stops
The skyward pinion winnowing through.
My trees shut out the world;—their tops
Are open to the infinite blue.

Where the Cattle Come to Drink

At evening, where the cattle come to drink,
Cool are the long marsh-grasses, dewy cool
The alder thickets, and the shallow pool,
And the brown clay about the trodden brink.
The pensive afterthoughts of sundown sink
Over the patient acres given to peace;
The homely cries and farmstead noises cease,
And the worn day relaxes, link by link.

A lesson that the open heart may read
Breathes in this mild benignity of air,
These dear, familiar savours of the soil,—
A lesson of the calm of humble creed,
The simple dignity of common toil,
And the plain wisdom of unspoken prayer.

An Epitaph for a Husbandman

He who would start and rise
Before the crowing cocks,—
No more he lifts his eyes,
Whoever knocks.

He who before the stars
Would call the cattle home,—
They wait about the bars
For him to come.

Him at whose hearty calls
The farmstead woke again
The horses in their stalls
Expect in vain.

Busy, and blithe, and bold,
He laboured for the morrow,—
The plough his hands would hold
Rusts in the furrow.

His fields he had to leave,
His orchards cool and dim;
The clods he used to cleave
Now cover him.

But the green, growing things
Lean kindly to his sleep,—
White roots and wandering strings,
Closer they creep.

Because he loved them long
And with them bore his part,
Tenderly now they throng
About his heart.

The Stillness of the Frost

Out of the frost-white wood comes winnowing through
No wing; no homely call or cry is heard.
Even the hope of life seems far deferred.
The hard hills ache beneath their spectral hue.
A dove-grey cloud, tender as tears or dew,
From one lone hearth exhaling, hangs unstirred,
Like the poised ghost of some unnamed great bird
In the ineffable pallor of the blue.

Such, I must think, even at the dawn of Time,
Was thy white hush, O world, when thou lay'st cold,
Unwaked to love, new from the Maker's word,

And the spheres, watching, stilled their high accord,
To marvel at perfection in thy mould,
The grace of thine austerity sublime!

The Brook in February

A snowy path for squirrel and fox,
It winds between the wintry firs.
Snow-muffled are its iron rocks,
And o'er its stillness nothing stirs.

But low, bend low a listening ear!
Beneath the mask of moveless white
A babbling whisper you shall hear—
Of birds and blossoms, leaves and light.

Twilight on Sixth Avenue

Over the tops of the houses
Twilight and sunset meet.
The green, diaphanous dusk
Sinks to the eager street.

Astray in the tangle of roofs
Wanders a wind of June.
The dial shines in the clock-tower
Like the face of a strange-scrawled moon.

The narrowing lines of the houses
Palely begin to gleam,
And the hurrying crowds fade softly
Like an army in a dream.

Above the vanishing faces
  A phantom train flares on
With a voice that shakes the shadows,—
  Diminishes, and is gone.

And I walk with the journeying throng
  In such a solitude
As where a lonely ocean
  Washes a lonely wood.

A Nocturne of Exile

Out of this night of lonely noise,
  The city's crowded cries,
Home of my heart, to thee, to thee
  I turn my longing eyes.

Years, years, how many years I went
  In exile wearily,
Before I lifted up my face
  And saw my home in thee.

I had come home to thee at last.
  I saw thy warm lights gleam.
I entered thine abiding joy,—
  Oh, was it but a dream?

Ere I could reckon with my heart
  The sum of our delight,
I was an exile once again
  Here in the hasting night.

Thy doors were shut; thy lights were gone
  From my remembering eyes.
Only the city's endless throng!
  Only the crowded cries!

At the Wayside Shrine

Ste. Anne De Beaupré

So little and so kind a shrine!
So homely and serene a saint!—
No violent sorrow can be thine,
Thou patient pensioner of constraint!

This gentle gloom that wraps thee in
Mistaking for a soul's despair,
Thou griev'st, perchance, for some small sin,
Too trivial for such fervent prayer.

Not sin hath wanned thy weary face,
Nor living woe made dark thine eyes,
Nor memory wrought this pleading grace,—
But ignorance, and dumb surmise.

The bleeding feet of shameful pain
Have passed not up this tranquil way,
Nor late repentance, haply vain,
By these slim poplars knelt to pray.

Thine is the sadness of the breast
That has not known the human strife—
Weighed down with shelter, worn with rest,
Athirst for the free storms of life.

Thine is the ache of lips that ache
For unknown pangs, unknown delight,—
The emptiness of hearts that break
With dreaming through the empty night.

Thy woe thou canst not understand,
Poor soul and body incomplete!
Thou hungerest for a little hand
And touch of little unknown feet.

But now, because all sorrows cease
Assuaged by such sweet faith as thine,
The dear Saint Anne shall give thee peace
Here at her little, kindly shrine.

John Frederic Herbin

The only Acadian among the Confederation Poets, John Frederic Herbin was born on February 8, 1860 in Windsor, Nova Scotia. Our poet's mother, Marie-Marguerite Robichaud, was a native Acadian; his father, John Herbin, was a Huguenot from Cambrai, France. Herbin identified with his mother's people, and he made the Acadian Diaspora (1755–1763) a major topic of his work in poetry, non-fiction, and fiction. The diaspora was, shamefully, an eighteenth century example of ethnic cleansing. To preserve the story of the Acadians and their suffering, Herbin was the prime force behind creating the Grand-Pré National Historic Site, today a UNESCO World Heritage Site.

Herbin chose to write in English, his most important poetical work being *The Marshlands and The Trail of the Tide* (1899). Herbin, however, was not simply a poet of the Acadian people and their struggles; he wrote a great deal of pure nature poetry, the focus of which was the Fundean marshes, their beauty and their history. In this regard, he was an Acadian version of Straton, Roberts, Carman, and Hensley—the "Singers of Minas" after the Minas Basin of the Bay of Fundy. Together, they put the Bay of Fundy on Canada's literary map. He lived his entire life on the Nova Scotian side of Fundy, dying on December 29, 1923 at Wolfville, Nova Scotia.

Across the Dykes

The dykes half bare are lying in the bath
Of quivering sunlight on this Sunday morn;
And bobolinks aflock make sweet the worn
Old places where two centuries of swath
Have fallen to earth before the mowers' path.
Across the dykes the bell's low sound is borne
From green Grand-Pré, abundant with the corn,
With milk and honey which it always hath.
And now I hear the Angelus ring far;
See faith bow many a head that suffered wrong
Near all these plains they wrested from the tide.
The visions of their last great sorrows mar
The greenness of these meadows; in the song
Of birds I feel a tear that has not dried.

A Rifled Grave at Grand-Pré

These silent chambers, which thy dead immure,
Have felt no changes with the changing land,
Until to-day when a rude foot did stand
Within thy narrow house, the grave not sure.
Yet with no name or age that might endure,
Thy mould is gathered to the kindly sand,
Safe from the touch of desecrating hand,
The shroud no guard nor blackened bones secure.
Kind Nature has absorbed thee as her own,
Sweet fate indeed to live no other fame,
To feel the tides and seasons in their flow.
Thy story is not bitter there alone
Without a place to mark thee now, no name,
Thy empty coffin for the soulless foe.

The Sea-Harvest

On the great sea-marsh where the eddies stray,
The mowers strike ere yet the dew is fled.
The salt-grass falls before their heavy tread,
Filling with odorous breath the whole green way.
On the tide's back, now with the broadened day,
Like a mild beast of burden slowly led,
The floating grass is meshed and gatherèd;
A great tide-harvest of salt-smelling hay.
Where herons stalk, and the shy mallard glides
In stillest haunts, is the man-worker seen;
Even the sea must garner for his good,
Till high and dark above the marsh and tides
Stand the great hay-towers, as they loom and lean,
Like turrets grim, to mark the solitude.

In the Gaspereau Valley

The rippling river ceased to sing, with flow
Quick-speeding downward to the red-shored Bay;
For now the tide has found the tortuous way
Between the hills where orchard blossoms blow;
And the green dykes and meadows are aglow
With th' even radiance of a golden day.
The waters' hush is strange; and the last lay
Of unseen cat-birds ripples to and fro.
The day is gone, and with a lingering hand
The sea's dark fingers press upon the shore.
The bat has risen into broken flight
Above the bridge, and darts from strand to strand.
The silence deepens over me; while more
And more I feel the fulness of the night.

The Broken Dyke

From the far ocean, hour after hour,
Inflowed the waveless and quick-rising flood;
Until the marsh-reeds like a storm-struck wood,
Beneath the murky waters curve and cower.
The tortuous dyke-wall, crowned of grass and flower,
That has a century of tides withstood,
Leans hard to-night against the sea-front rude,
Awaiting the great current's fullest power.
In vain the strength and virtue of its years!
O'er fence and furrow, through the broken walls,
Across the verdant fields, the tide has thrown
Its torrent arms; and the awed listener hears
Through the deep night the herds' harsh cries and calls,
As the fierce ocean leaps to claim its own.

The Acadian Exile

Where are the hands to guide the waiting plow;
To sway the lumbering oxen with a stroke,
Now waiting at the bars for band or yoke?
An exile curst, as with a branded brow.
The kindly walls that cannot shield him now
Are black in embers that have ceased to smoke,
Wrapt tenderly with marsh-fogs as a cloak.
The willows shade no gables where they bow.
This wandering exile from dead Acadie
Sees through the mist of sorrow never done
That mercy has no hand held out to save.
Yet ne'er again the meadows of the sea
Mayhap shall know this heart-sore, weary son,
Denied the kindness of an alien grave.

A Homestead

Winter

I found the fullest days of summer here
    Between these sloping meadow-hills and yon;
    And came all beauty then from dawn to dawn,
Whether the tide was veiled or flowing clear.
To-day in snowy raiment nowise drear
    Thou liest peaceful, as with hair undone,
    And every jewel aside. Thou dreamest on,
Soon to be waked by the new-flowering year.
Old trees and walks will never make thee old,
    For years add beauty to a peaceful age.
        Thou art amidst all change the same, and strong;
Crowning the whole broad view that lies outrolled:
    The mountain and the sea thy heritage
        To keep thee beautiful, to keep thee young.

Change

The early crows slow down the dyke-lands fly,
    A sombre troop upon the heels of dawn;
While fog-thick breezes dim the morning sky,
    Dark with the trailing skirts of night just gone.

The drowse of dawn clings to the early hours,
    To the neglected scenes and gardens bare,
So fragrant late with plenteousness of flowers,
    Now scant of bloom, and silent everywhere.

The tide flows seaward as the day expands,
    And the slow Autumn waking fills the day;
And when the fallen flood rolls from the sands
    There is no sign of languor or decay.

The season reigns with the soft calm of rest
O'er the whole marshland in the sun's full rays.
Each night that earlier floods the golden west,
Each dallying dawn, comes with a newer phase.

When from the west comes a soft flood of airs,
And brims the land with subtle charms and sweet,
Then Nature's quiet wanes with all her cares,
And Autumn glorious roves with laughing feet.

She lingers long with Night, and bends her eyes,
With every sun returning, to the north,
Expectant of the white-clad cavalries,
And wan and wistful waits their coming forth.

She stills the waking bud and reds the thorn,
And dyes the forest with a single sweep;
She looks upon the eyes of languid Morn,
And makes her coming late and calm her sleep.

Oft are the raging winds upon the plains,
Breathing decay upon the dulling land;
And wafting fogs, like cold unfallen rains,
Come with the tides upon the birdless sand.

The woods are stricken, and the parting song
Of birds yet lingers on the misty dawn.
The lakes are waveless-black the hills among,
And stiller since the laughing loon has flown.

But with the night again, through all its hours,
The waft of a cold wind sweeps o'er the woods;
And morning breezes thick with leafy showers
Strew field and forest, and bedeck the floods.

Like thin-draped Poverty with bending form
  Scarce hid beneath the tatters of her dress,
Appear the willows moaning in the storm,
  Unpitied in their shivering nakedness.

Again the night's far sky is bright with stars,
  But a cold trance has stilled the breeze's breath.
Beneath the morn all stricken unawares
  Lies the whole land in sombre robe of death.

What need of shade along these waysides now,
  Of arching boughs, and eye-delighting green?
No longer noon-day burns the laborer's brow;
  Bare are the vacant fields of fruit and sheen.

The harvest-day has left the orchards bare;
  The nights are longer, and the sun runs low.
The eager hunter for the chase prepares,
  To seek the forest with the moon's full glow.

The lofty hawk no longer meets the night,
  Cutting the twilight with a noiseless wing.
About the spire no swallow curves in flight,
  On calm, fruit-smelling airs of evening.

The gloaming has no bat, the gloom is dead;
  No dreaming bird trills short a midnight-lay.
The heavens hang with frozen stars o'erhead,
  And chill until the coming of the day.

Where laughter rolls along the frozen lake
  The woods have lost the silence and the gloom.
While youthful blood is flowing joy will wake
  Beside the sign of death and touch of doom.

The time was good; the land may calmly rest
  When Winter wanders through the silent ways.
The warmth of life again will move her breast,
  To waken and restore in other days.

The seasons live their days of loss and gain—
  Mild Spring like youth, and Summer like a queen;
Ripe Autumn has a brief and changeful reign
  Ere Winter's snowy mantle sweeps the green.

These changes point to work that should be done,
  And tell the sower where he cast in vain—
Beginnings end if well or ill begun,
  And with the thistle falls the ripened grain.

Restoration

We stand, sweet love, beside the scattered stones
  That mark where once a hearth and home have stood;
  Acadian happiness that felt the rude
And ruthless blow of hate. There lie the bones,
Mayhap, of my own kindred, whence the tones
  Of leafy willows come; and yonder stand
  The apple-trees they set with careful hand;
While every marsh their dyking labor owns.
Now here our love forgives the hateful deed;
  Forgetting not a sorrow nor a pain;
    Recalling each dark page sadder than tears,
For love is reigning where their lives did bleed.
  Their loss was all; yet here my life does gain
    Its joyous good for all the other years.

The Tide-Line

There was a tide last night, gone out to-day
Into the blue sea-reaches, and it played
With dallying touch or often roughly laid
Its strength upon the shore to rend and slay.
In varying mood the line's long curving way
Discloses where his wandering foot was stayed,
Only at rocky rampart steep to fade,
The sea's triumphal tread around the bay.
The seaweed dying in the sun's full light;
A shell left helpless, like a spoken thought
Meant in the secret of the heart to shine;
And the shaped wood of ship whose living light
Went down somewhere—aye, many a thing I caught
Both sad and glad along the tidal-line.

Stone Ripple-Marks

Beneath a cliff wrenched from the inner earth,
All seamed and dark from elemental war,
I saw rich crystals marking many a scar,
Made when the earth was recent from its birth.
I read the first bare pages of her dearth
In long wave ripples of a sandstone bar,
Formed when the cycles learned to make and mar;
A rocky page of story here set forth.
I held a fossil reptile in my hand,
Till now unseen. And then there came to me
An echoed song through myriad years unsung.
And what is time, I thought, when I may stand
Beside the tracings of a former sea;
Live in the murmur of the wind yet young!

To Minas

Minas, storied with a people's woe,
Forever to be linked with their distress,
Thou hast deep wisdom in the bitterness
And joy of life. And ever ebb and flow
My soul-floods with thy tides that come and go.
My stronger life sprang from thy red largess,
And thy green deeps and ceaseless might no less
Did calm my love and deeper hope bestow.
Thou wast the Mentor of my singing dawn,
Laving my lips, and mixing with my blood;
I have no year that is not tinged with thee.
Voiced with thy deep concordance, living on
To ebb thy strength and rise like all thy flood,
My soul must also feed upon the sea.

Blomidon

Dark was thy coming, and with fire and dearth;
Internal shudderings and voiceless throes;
When from the burning depths thy form arose
To lie all black and shapeless on the earth;
To span the seas afar as with a girth,
Moveless before the mighty tidal blows,
Girding the valleys for a long repose,
Till life should vaguely long and come to birth.
O patient greatness of a slow pursuit,
The purpose of a hundred centuries,
Clothed with the forest glory and green plains;
Thy rock now sleeps beneath the spreading root
And mould of ages; and a splendor skies
Thee, child of earth, now laid in flowery chains.

Seining

The broadened flats go glimmering to the sea,
  And the great net that struggled with the tide
  Hangs dark and moveless, for the winds have died;
On high the circling gulls cry ceaselessly.
A horse goes slowly sinking to the knee
  In the red earth, dragging with dart and glide
  The mud-boat after on the trackless, wide
Shore level to the sein's day fishery.
Again, beneath the stars down by the seas,
  Dark, sobbing tide-waves slip through span on span
    Of net, quick bared and curving like a wing.
Night labor now companioned by the breeze,
  The glowing lantern glides to where for man
    The harvest of the sea is garnering.

Helena Coleman

Helena Jane Coleman was born on April 27, 1860 near the Bay of Quinte in Newcastle, Ontario. She was the last of our Confederation Poets to publish a book; her *Songs and Sonnets* was issued under the auspices of The Tennyson Club of Toronto in 1906. While there are many fine poems included in this initial offering, Coleman is perhaps better known for her *Marching Men: War Verses* (1917). She also served as head of the music department of the Ontario Ladies' College.

Coleman was physically disabled, having suffered from polio, and her "Give Me No Pity" is perhaps the first Canadian poem dealing directly with disability. Despite facing discrimination due to her handicap—she walked awkwardly with crutches, and later used a wheelchair—she overcame all barriers to have her poetry published via the prestigious Tennyson Club. Her poems of the First World War rank high among those rooted in that traumatic conflict. She died on December 7, 1953 at Toronto, Ontario.

Give Me No Pity

Destroy me not, O friend, I pray,
With thy well-meaning sympathy;
Give me no pity, but a place
Where falls the sunlight on my face.

The race is to the swift, I know,
The battle to the strong; but Oh!
Full recompense there is for each
When Heaven itself is in our reach.

The widow's gift of old was small,
Yet was it counted more than all;
'Tis what he does, not what he can,
That proves the measure of the man.

And so, if thou would'st have me strong,
Dwell not on what is sad or wrong;
'Tis not in marking how they fail
That men find courage to prevail.

I ask no more than just the chance
To match my will with circumstance,
With what I am in mind and heart
To take my due and play my part.

God showeth me no special grace,
And why should'st thou? Yield me my place—
The right to strive—and spare me, pray,
Thy well-intentioned sympathy.

I am Content with Canada

Of countries far and famed have I been told,
　And of the joys that foreign travel brings,
Of wonders, beauties one would fain behold
　To stir the heart with fresh imaginings.

And I myself in storied Switzerland
　Have watched the Alps in their majestic calm,
And been by jasmine-scented breezes fanned
　In tropic isles that bear the stately palm.

And many a fabled castle on the Rhine
　Has winged my fancy as we drifted by;
Beside the oleander and the vine
　I've dreamed beneath the soft Italian sky.

But I have never been more deeply stirred
　By any loveliness of land or sea
Than when upon Canadian shores I've heard
　The lonely loon or curlew call to me

Across our own unnumbered Northern lakes,
　And over leagues of winding water-ways
Upon whose nameless shores the aspen shakes
　And yellows in the soft autumnal haze.

(And O to swing away where all is new,
　And share the haunts of shy and tameless things,
To dip one's paddle in the liquid blue
　And skim the water lightly as with wings!)

When on the broad St. Lawrence some gray day,
　Among those islands wrought of mist and dreams,
I drift to realms of unreality
　Where all the world a lovely vision seems;

Or when among the Rockies I have caught
  The sudden gleam of peaks above the cloud,
And on the tumult of my quickened thought
  New visions, dreams and aspirations crowd;

Or, thinking of the future and of all
  That generations yet unborn shall see—
The forests that for axe and ploughshare call,
  The wealth of golden harvests yet to be,

I am content with Canada, and ask
  No fairer land than has been given me,
No greater joy, no more inspiring task,
  Than to upbuild and share her destiny.

Love's Seasons

When first you came, it was perpetual Spring,
Fourfold of rapture flamed in everything,
And all abroad the gods went wandering.

Then followed Summer, full, luxuriant;
We wrought together, and our days were spent
In love's fulfilment and life's sacrament.

'Tis Autumn now, and all that went before—
The joy of Spring, the Summer's golden store—
We harvest in our hearts to fail no more.

To fail no more? When winter storms must sweep
Across the shrines where we were wont to keep
Love's sacred tryst, and soon—so soon shall sleep?

Yea, Love, whate'er betide, I know the seed
Of what was wrought in faithful love and deed
Shall but lie dormant waiting higher need.

The Guardians of the Place

About the old deserted place,
    So long forsaken and forlorn,
There lingers still a touch of grace,
    A fragrance every year new-born.

For lilacs there in Spring unfold
    Beside the long unopened door,
Communion still they seem to hold
    With those who come and go no more.

Against the window-frame they lean,
    Their banners floating to the air,
And spread their arms as if to screen
    The silent shadows lurking there.

Pale spires uplifted to the sun
    Break into bloom as if to fill,
In memory of days long done,
    The empty place with fragrance still.

As if with beauty they would hide
    The fallen fortunes of the race,
Still cherishing with love and pride
    The old traditions of the place.

So year by year they closer press,
    And every season slowly spread,
Praising with silent loveliness
    The unknown, long-forgotten dead.

The Voices of Our Day

How shall we bring to one clear tone
    The divers voices of our day,
    Or what authority obey
Where tongues arise, confused, unknown?

How shall we in the clamor give
    To each an undivided ear,
    Or through discordant doctrines hear
The still, small voice imperative?

Where devious roadways twist and cross
    How shall we find the narrow way
    That leads afar to endless day,
Past all this fevered fret and loss?

Can doubting spirits ever thrust
    Their roots deep to the heart of life?
    Or bear above its toil and strife
The fruit of steadfast love and trust?

When in the wilderness we roam,
    And from afar strange voices call,
    And night's uncertain shadows fall,
How shall we know which way leads home?

When Autumn Comes

When Spring first breathes on the russet hill,
    In her own faint, lovely fashion,
One's pulses stir with a sudden thrill;
But when Autumn comes the heart stands still,
    Moved with a deeper passion.

There's a wonderful charm in the soft, still days
When earth to her rest is returning,
When the hills are drowned in a purple haze,
When the wild grape sweetens, and all in a blaze
Of crimson the maples are turning.

Open thy gates, O heart of mine!
These are the days we have waited,
Put to thy lips the draught divine,
These are the days that hold the wine
Of Summer concentrated.

Night Among the Thousand Islands

Mysterious falls the moon's transforming light
On lichen-covered rock and granite wall,
Comes piercing through the hollows of the night
The loon's weird, plaintive call.

Like some great regiment upon the shore
The stalwart pines go trooping up the hill,
And faintly in the distance o'er and o'er
Echoes the whip-poor-will.

Like silhouettes the dreaming islands keep
Their silent watches, mirrored in the tide,
While in their labyrinthine aisles some deep,
Still mystery seems to hide.

From out the shadows dim against the sky
Come stealing shadow-ships not made of men,
Faint phantom-barques that slowly drifting by
Are swallowed up again.

While silently beneath, the river flows,
  Unfathomed, dark, a great restless tide,
Within its bosom deep the virgin snows
    From many a mountain-side.

And, drifting with the current, how we feel
  The haunting witchery of Beauty's spell!
The world we left behind seems all unreal,
    Where such enchantments dwell.

The vexing cares that overfill our days
  Slip stealthily away, and we are wooed
Back to the healing, half-forgotten ways
    Of peace and solitude.

In October

On the university lawn

Touched by October's changing frost and heat,
  The ivy flames upon the gray old walls,
  Or, whirled by sudden, fitful breezes, falls
In little crimson showers at our feet;
Impetuous Spring and lingering Autumn meet
  On these wide lawns and in the echoing halls,
  For Summer with its golden bounty calls
To hearts that still with youth and promise beat.

These Norman towers uplifted to the sun
  A nation's hope enshrine, a nation's pride,
And one can scarcely look unmoved upon
  The nation's youth now gathering to their side,
So great the future to be lost or won—
  So sweet the siren-songs, so swift the tide!

At Sunset

From green to gold, from gold to amethyst,
  Transmuted by the sun's last lingering ray,
  The tranquil hills in dreaming silence lay,
Wrought to a beauty eye could not resist;
Till, folded in with veils of purple mist
  That slowly wrapt them from reluctant day,
  They mingled with the dusk and flowed away,
Renewing with the stars their nightly tryst.

And as the soft enchantments round us spread,
  And twilight with its pensive shadows fell—
Loosed from the prison-wards of care and dread,
  Lured from our selfish griefs by beauty's spell—
Along dim thoroughfares our thoughts were led
  To haunts of peace where love and silence dwell.

Night

Who hath not in the silences of night
  Been humbled by the mystery that lies
  Along the vaulted pathway of the skies?
And in the consciousness that worlds of light
Their steadfast courses keep beyond our sight,
  Heard yet again the voice within that cries
  To every fettered soul, bidding it rise
With arms outstretched towards the Infinite?

Upon the threshold of these large, unknown,
  Unlighted chambers of the night we kneel,
And, emptied of the day, contrite, alone,
    The presence of some sentient Power within
  The magnitudes of space we dimly feel
    To which the finite spirit is akin.

The Evening Hour

There is unfailing comfort to be found
 In quiet country ways when shadows run
 Athwart green pastures with the setting sun,
And coming harvests everywhere abound;
The singing streams half-hidden in the ground,
 The orchard slopes, the kine that one by one
 Go home for milking now the day is done,
All speak of homes with peace and plenty crowned.

More reconciling thoughts come to the mind
 At such an hour; we feel the recompense
Of honest toil—draw nearer to our kind
 In spiritual sympathy, and in the sense
Of some enfolding Care that dwells behind
 The fixed, dividing walls of circumstance.

The Day He Went

The morning dawned both bright and clear,
 That unforgotten day he went,
The hills were blue and very near
 As if for their encouragement.

The rose that was her special care,
 Had come to color over night,
And lifted to the radiant air
 A bud half-blown—a lovely sight.

He paused a moment by its side,
 Their mingling glances on it fell,
Then his roamed where the hills divide,
 Taking of them a mute farewell.

He swept the horizon half around,
Standing erect with kindling eye
That rested where the slope pine-crowned
Went climbing up to meet the sky.

And then to her—with one deep look
That knit her spirit to his own,
Courage and strength of him she took,
And heart to face the road alone.

No word was said; the years behind
Held no regret; and each to each
Gave pledge of what their souls divined
Better in silence than in speech.

And They Were Young

'Tis when you're young and life ascends
That joy waits where the white road bends,
And every face you meet is a friend's.

'Tis when you're young that dreams come true,
And never a cloud but the sun shines through,
When life holds out both hands to you.

For youth it is that rainbows gleam
With showers of gold in every beam—
At either end a pot o' dream.

Ever for youth the roads run straight,
And out beside the wishing-gate
Fairies and blindfold fortune wait.

For youth the jealous roses keep
Their red hearts closed in reticence deep—
The lilies wait in folded sleep.

And oh, for youth each bush with God
Is still afire, and every sod
Bears imprint where His foot has trod.

And they were young who lie so still
Far on that sodden Flanders hill.

Autumn, 1917

We know by many a tender token
When Indian-Summer days have come,
By rustling leaves in branches oaken
And by the cricket's sleepy hum.

By aspen leaves no longer shaken,
And by the river's silvered thread,
The oriole's swinging cup forsaken,
Emptied of music overhead.

By long slant lines on field and fallow,
By mellowing portals of the wood,
By silences that seem to hallow
And invite to solitude…

Are there young hearts in France recalling
These dream-filled, blue Canadian days,
When gold and scarlet flames are falling
From beech and maple set ablaze?

Pluck they again the pale, wild aster,
The bending plume of golden-rod?
And do their exiled hearts beat faster
Roaming in thought their native sod?

Dream they of Canada crowned and golden,
    Flushed with her Autumn diadem?
In years to come when time is olden,
    Canada's dream shall be of them—

Shall be of them who gave for others
    The ardour of their radiant years;—
Your name in Canada's heart, my brothers,
    Shall be remembered long with tears!

We give you vision back for vision,
    Forgetting not the price you paid,
O bearers of the world's decision,
    On whom the nation's debt was laid.

No heart can view these highways glowing
    With gold transmuted from the clod,
But crowns your glorious manhood, knowing
    You gave us back our faith in God.

Convocation Hall

May 18th, 1917

They rose,
The honored and the grave,
The reverend, the grey,
While one read out the names of those
Who, gallant, young and brave,
Upon the field of battle gave
Their ardent lives away.

They rose to honor Youth—
What honor could they give?
What tribute shall we lay
Who still in safety live?
Before the shrine of those who pay
The price of honor and of truth
Giving their lives away?

They rose in reverence, yea;
But those who lie
Far on the Flanders field to-day
Had not an answering word to say;
Their silence thundered their reply—
They gave their lives away!

E. Pauline Johnson (Tekahionwake)

Emily Pauline Johnson, whose Mohawk name was Tekahionwake, was born on March 10, 1861 on the Six Nations Reserve, located near Brantford, Ontario. Her father, George H.M. Johnson, was the Head Chief, and thus she was a "Mohawk princess," a role she made use of in public presentations of her poetry in Canada, the United States, and Britain. Her mother was Emily Howells, an English woman from Bristol. It was her mother who introduced the young girl to the joys of British literature, and Johnson's first poetry collection, *The White Wampum*, was published in London in 1895 by The Bodley Head. An auspicious start.

Her themes included the relationship between different tribes of Indigenous Peoples, the conflicts engendered for Indigenous Peoples by life in a White-dominated world, the tensions that arise in a woman living in a male-dominated world, and, like other Confederation Poets, the grand and varied natural beauty of Canada, from Halifax to Vancouver. Although she was sickly from birth, her poetry displayed, above all, a faith in and a hope for Canada's future. Despite her books of poetry and fiction, and despite her popular and well-attended reading tours, Johnson died in poverty, supported by the charity of her friends, on March 7, 1913 at Vancouver, British Columbia.

As Red Men Die

Captive! Is there a hell to him like this?
A taunt more galling than the Huron's hiss?
He—proud and scornful, he—who laughed at law,
He—scion of the deadly Iroquois,
He—the bloodthirsty, he—the Mohawk chief,
He—who despises pain and sneers at grief,
Here in the hated Huron's vicious clutch,
That even captive he disdains to touch!

Captive! But *never* conquered; Mohawk brave
Stoops not to be to *any* man a slave;
Least, to the puny tribe his soul abhors,
The tribe whose wigwams sprinkle Simcoe's shores.
With scowling brow he stands and courage high,
Watching with haughty and defiant eye
His captors, as they council o'er his fate,
Or strive his boldness to intimidate.
Then fling they unto him the choice;
"Wilt thou
Walk o'er the bed of fire that waits thee now—
Walk with uncovered feet upon the coals,
Until thou reach the ghostly Land of Souls,
And, with thy Mohawk death-song please our ear?
Or wilt thou with the women rest thee here?"
His eyes flash like an eagle's, and his hands
Clench at the insult. Like a god he stands.
"Prepare the fire!" he scornfully demands.

He knoweth not that this same jeering band
Will bite the dust—will lick the Mohawk's hand;
Will kneel and cower at the Mohawk's feet;
Will shrink when Mohawk war drums wildly beat.

His death will be avenged with hideous hate
By Iroquois, swift to annihilate
His vile detested captors, that now flaunt
Their war clubs in his face with sneer and taunt,
Not thinking, soon that reeking, red, and raw,
Their scalps will deck the belts of Iroquois.

The path of coals outstretches, white with heat,
A forest fir's length—ready for his feet.
Unflinching as a rock he steps along
The burning mass, and sings his wild war song;
Sings, as he sang when once he used to roam
Throughout the forests of his southern home,
Where, down the Genesee, the water roars,
Where gentle Mohawk purls between its shores,
Songs, that of exploit and of prowess tell;
Songs of the Iroquois invincible.

Up the long trail of fire he boasting goes,
Dancing a war dance to defy his foes.
His flesh is scorched, his muscles burn and shrink,
But still he dances to death's awful brink.
The eagle plume that crests his haughty head
Will *never* droop until his heart be dead.
Slower and slower yet his footstep swings,
Wilder and wilder still his death-song rings,
Fiercer and fiercer thro' the forest bounds
His voice that leaps to Happier Hunting Grounds.
One savage yell—

Then loyal to his race,
He bends to death—but *never* to disgrace.

A Cry from an Indian Wife

My forest brave, my Red-skin love, farewell;
We may not meet to-morrow; who can tell
What mighty ills befall our little band,
Or what you'll suffer from the white man's hand?
Here is your knife! I thought 'twas sheathed for aye.
No roaming bison calls for it to-day;
No hide of prairie cattle will it maim;
The plains are bare, it seeks a nobler game:
'Twill drink the life-blood of a soldier host.
Go; rise and strike, no matter what the cost.
Yet stay. Revolt not at the Union Jack,
Nor raise Thy hand against this stripling pack
Of white-faced warriors, marching West to quell
Our fallen tribe that rises to rebel.
They all are young and beautiful and good;
Curse to the war that drinks their harmless blood.
Curse to the fate that brought them from the East
To be our chiefs—to make our nation least
That breathes the air of this vast continent.
Still their new rule and council is well meant.
They but forget we Indians owned the land
From ocean unto ocean; that they stand
Upon a soil that centuries agone
Was our sole kingdom and our right alone.
They never think how they would feel to-day,
If some great nation came from far away,
Wresting their country from their hapless braves,
Giving what they gave us—but wars and graves.
Then go and strike for liberty and life,
And bring back honour to your Indian wife.
Your wife? Ah, what of that, who cares for me?
Who pities my poor love and agony?
What white-robed priest prays for your safety here,

As prayer is said for every volunteer
That swells the ranks that Canada sends out?
Who prays for vict'ry for the Indian scout?
Who prays for our poor nation lying low?
None—therefore take your tomahawk and go.
My heart may break and burn into its core,
But I am strong to bid you go to war.
Yet stay, my heart is not the only one
That grieves the loss of husband and of son;
Think of the mothers o'er the inland seas;
Think of the pale-faced maiden on her knees;
One pleads her God to guard some sweet-faced child
That marches on toward the North-West wild.
The other prays to shield her love from harm,
To strengthen his young, proud uplifted arm.
Ah, how her white face quivers thus to think,
Your tomahawk his life's best blood will drink.
She never thinks of my wild aching breast,
Nor prays for your dark face and eagle crest
Endangered by a thousand rifle balls,
My heart the target if my warrior falls.
O! coward self I hesitate no more;
Go forth, and win the glories of the war.
Go forth, nor bend to greed of white men's hands,
By right, by birth we Indians own these lands,
Though starved, crushed, plundered, lies our nation low ...
Perhaps the white man's God has willed it so.

Shadow River

Muskoka

A stream of tender gladness,
Of filmy sun, and opal tinted skies;
Of warm midsummer air that lightly lies
In mystic rings,
Where softly swings
The music of a thousand wings
That almost tones to sadness.

Midway 'twixt earth and heaven,
A bubble in the pearly air, I seem
To float upon the sapphire floor, a dream
Of clouds of snow,
Above, below,
Drift with my drifting, dim and slow,
As twilight drifts to even.

The little fern-leaf, bending
Upon the brink, its green reflection greets,
And kisses soft the shadow that it meets
With touch so fine,
The border line
The keenest vision can't define;
So perfect is the blending.

The far, fir trees that cover
The brownish hills with needles green and gold,
The arching elms o'erhead, vinegrown and old,
Repictured are
Beneath me far,
Where not a ripple moves to mar
Shades underneath, or over.

Mine is the undertone;
The beauty, strength, and power of the land
Will never stir or bend at my command;
But all the shade
Is marred or made,
If I but dip my paddle blade;
And it is mine alone,

O! pathless world of seeming!
O! pathless life of mine whose deep ideal
Is more my own than ever was the real.
For others Fame
And Love's red flame,
And yellow gold; I only claim
The shadows and the dreaming.

Re-voyage

What of the days when we two dreamed together?
    Days marvellously fair,
As lightsome as a skyward floating feather
    Sailing on summer air—
Summer, summer, that came drifting through
Fate's hand to me, to you.

What of the days, my dear? I sometimes wonder
    If you too wish this sky
Could be the blue we sailed so softly under,
    In that sun-kissed July;
Sailed in the warm and yellow afternoon,
With hearts in touch and tune.

Have you no longing to re-live the dreaming,
    Adrift in my canoe?
To watch my paddle blade all wet and gleaming
    Cleaving the waters through?
To lie wind-blown and wave-caressed, until
Your restless pulse grows still?

Do you not long to listen to the purling
    Of foam athwart the keel?
To hear the nearing rapids softly swirling
    Among their stones, to feel
The boat's unsteady tremor as it braves
The wild and snarling waves?

What need of question, what of your replying?
    Oh! well I know that you
Would toss the world away to be but lying
    Again in my canoe,
In listless indolence entranced and lost,
Wave-rocked, and passion tossed.

Ah me! my paddle failed me in the steering
    Across love's shoreless seas;
All reckless, I had ne'er a thought of fearing
    Such dreary days as these,
When through the self-same rapids we dash by,
My lone canoe and I.

Brier

Good Friday

Because, dear Christ, your tender, wounded arm
    Bends back the brier that edges life's long way
That no hurt comes to heart, to soul no harm,
    I do not feel the thorns so much to-day.

Because I never knew your care to tire,
    Your hand to weary guiding me aright,
Because you walk before and crush the brier,
    It does not pierce my feet so much to-night.

Because so often you have hearkened to
    My selfish prayers, I ask but one thing now,
That these harsh hands of mine add not unto
    The crown of thorns upon your bleeding brow.

Nocturne

Night of Mid-June, in heavy vapours dying,
Like priestly hands thy holy touch is lying
Upon the world's wide brow;
God-like and grand all nature is commanding
The "peace that passes human understanding";
I, also, feel it now.

What matters it to-night, if one life treasure
I covet, is not mine! Am I to measure
The gifts of Heaven's decree
By my desires? O! life for ever longing
For some far gift, where many gifts are thronging,
God wills, it may not be.

Am I to learn that longing, lifted higher,
Perhaps will catch the gleam of sacred fire
That shows my cross is gold?
That underneath this cross—however lowly,
A jewel rests, white, beautiful and holy,
Whose worth can not be told.

Like to a scene I watched one day in wonder:—
A city, great and powerful, lay under
A sky of grey and gold;
The sun outbreaking in his farewell hour,
Was scattering afar a yellow shower
Of light, that aureoled

With brief hot touch, so marvellous and shining,
A hundred steeples on the sky out-lining,
Like network threads of fire;
Above them all, with halo far outspreading,
I saw a golden cross in glory heading
A consecrated spire:

I only saw its gleaming form uplifting,
Against the clouds of grey to seaward drifting,
And yet I surely know
Beneath the seen, a great unseen is resting,
For while the cross that pinnacle is cresting,
An Altar lies below.

• • • • • • •

Night of Mid-June, so slumberous and tender,
Night of Mid-June, transcendent in thy splendour
Thy silent wings enfold
And hush my longing, as at thy desire
All colour fades from round that far-off spire,
Except its cross of gold.

Harvest Time

Pillowed and hushed on the silent plain,
Wrapped in her mantle of golden grain,

Wearied of pleasuring weeks away,
Summer is lying asleep to-day,—

Where winds come sweet from the wild-rose briers
And the smoke of the far-off prairie fires;

Yellow her hair as the goldenrod,
And brown her cheeks as the prairie sod;

Purple her eyes as the mists that dream
At the edge of some laggard sun-drowned stream;

But over their depths the lashes sweep,
For Summer is lying to-day asleep.

The north wind kisses her rosy mouth,
His rival frowns in the far-off south,

And comes caressing her sunburnt cheek,
And Summer awakes for one short week,—

Awakes and gathers her wealth of grain,
Then sleeps and dreams for a year again.

Low Tide at St. Andrews

New Brunswick

The long red flats stretch open to the sky,
Breathing their moisture on the August air.
The seaweeds cling with flesh-like fingers where
The rocks give shelter that the sands deny;
And wrapped in all her summer harmonies
St. Andrews sleeps beside her sleeping seas.

The far-off shores swim blue and indistinct,
Like half-lost memories of some old dream.
The listless waves that catch each sunny gleam
Are idling up the waterways land-linked,
And, yellowing along the harbour's breast,
The light is leaping shoreward from the west.

And naked-footed children, tripping down,
Light with young laughter, daily come at eve
To gather dulse and sea clams and then heave
Their loads, returning laden to the town,
Leaving a strange grey silence when they go,—
The silence of the sands when tides are low.

Silhouette

The sky-line melts from the russet into blue,
Unbroken the horizon, saving where
A wreath of smoke curls up the far, thin air,
And points the distant lodges of the Sioux.

Etched where the lands and cloudlands touch and die
A solitary Indian tepee stands,
The only habitation of these lands,
That roll their magnitude from sky to sky.

The tent poles lift and loom in thin relief,
The upward floating smoke ascends between,
And near the open doorway, gaunt and lean,
And shadow-like, there stands an Indian Chief.

With eyes that lost their lustre long ago,
With visage fixed and stern as fate's decree,
He looks towards the empty west, to see
The never-coming herd of buffalo.

Only the bones that bleach upon the plains,
Only the fleshless skeletons that lie
In ghastly nakedness and silence, cry
Out mutely that naught else to him remains.

The Sleeping Giant

Thunder Bay, Lake Superior

When did you sink to your dreamless sleep
    Out there in your thunder bed?
Where the tempests sweep,
And the waters leap,
    And the storms rage overhead.

Were you lying there on your couch alone
    Ere Egypt and Rome were born?
Ere the Age of Stone,
Or the world had known
    The Man with the Crown of Thorn.

The winds screech down from the open west,
And the thunders beat and break
On the amethyst
Of your rugged breast,—
But you never arise or wake.

You have locked your past, and you keep the key
In your heart 'neath the westing sun,
Where the mighty sea
And its shores will be
Storm-swept till the world is done.

At Crow's Nest Pass

At Crow's Nest Pass the mountains rend
Themselves apart, the rivers wend
A lawless course about their feet,
And breaking into torrents beat
In useless fury where they blend
At Crow's Nest Pass.

The nesting eagle, wise, discreet,
Wings up the gorge's lone retreat
And makes some barren crag her friend
At Crow's Nest Pass.

Uncertain clouds, half-high, suspend
Their shifting vapours, and contend
With rocks that suffer not defeat;
And snows, and suns, and mad winds meet
To battle where the cliffs defend
At Crow's Nest Pass.

"Give Us Barabbas"

There was a man—a Jew of kingly blood,
  But of the people—poor and lowly born,
Accused of blasphemy of God, He stood
  Before the Roman Pilate, while in scorn
The multitude demanded it was fit
  That one should suffer for the people, while
Another be released, absolved, acquit,
  To live his life out virtuous or vile.

"Whom will ye have—Barabbas or this Jew?"
  Pilate made answer to the mob, "The choice
Is yours; I wash my hands of this, and you,
  Do as you will." With one vast ribald voice
The populace arose and, shrieking, cried,
  "Give us Barabbas, we condone his deeds!"
And He of Nazareth was crucified—
  Misjudged, condemned, dishonoured for their needs.

And down these nineteen centuries anew
  Comes the hoarse-throated, brutalized refrain,
"Give us Barabbas, crucify the Jew!"
  Once more a man must bear a nation's stain,—
And that in France, the chivalrous, whose lore
  Made her the flower of knightly age gone by.
Now she lies hideous with a leprous sore
  No skill can cure—no pardon purify.

And an indignant world, transfixed with hate
  Of such disease, cries, as in Herod's time,
Pointing its finger at her festering state,
  "Room for the leper, and her leprous crime!"
And France, writhing from years of torment, cries
  Out in her anguish, "Let this Jew endure,
Damned and disgraced, vicarious sacrifice.
  The honour of my army is secure."

And, vampire-like, that army sucks the blood
From out a martyr's veins, and strips his crown
Of honour from him, and his herohood
Flings in the dust, and cuts his manhood down.
Hide from your God, O! ye that did this act!
With lesser crimes the halls of Hell are paved.
Your army's honour may be still intact,
Unstained, unsoiled, unspotted,—but unsaved.

**Written after Dreyfus was exiled.*

Fire-flowers

And only where the forest fires have sped,
Scorching relentlessly the cool north lands,
A sweet wild flower lifts its purple head,
And, like some gentle spirit sorrow-fed,
It hides the scars with almost human hands.

And only to the heart that knows of grief,
Of desolating fire, of human pain,
There comes some purifying sweet belief,
Some fellow-feeling beautiful, if brief.
And life revives, and blossoms once again.

The Indian Corn Planter

He needs must leave the trapping and the chase,
For mating game his arrows ne'er despoil,
And from the hunter's heaven turn his face,
To wring some promise from the dormant soil.

He needs must leave the lodge that wintered him,
  The enervating fires, the blanket bed—
The women's dulcet voices, for the grim
  Realities of labouring for bread.

So goes he forth beneath the planter's moon
  With sack of seed that pledges large increase,
His simple pagan faith knows night and noon,
  Heat, cold, seedtime and harvest shall not cease.

And yielding to his needs, this honest sod,
  Brown as the hand that tills it, moist with rain,
Teeming with ripe fulfilment, true as God,
  With fostering richness, mothers every grain.

The Cattle Country

Up the dusk-enfolded prairie,
  Foot-falls, soft and sly,
Velvet cushioned, wild and wary,
  Then—the coyote's cry.

Rush of hoofs, and roar and rattle,
  Beasts of blood and breed,
Twenty thousand frightened cattle,
  Then—the wild stampede.

Pliant lasso circling wider
  In the frenzied flight—
Loping horse and cursing rider,
  Plunging through the night.

Rim of dawn the darkness losing
  Trail of blackened soil;
Perfume of the sage brush oozing
  On the air like oil.

Foothills to the Rockies lifting
  Brown, and blue, and green,
Warm Alberta sunlight drifting
  Over leagues between.

That's the country of the ranges,
  Plain and prairie land,
And the God who never changes
  Holds it in His hand.

The Train Dogs

Out of the night and the north;
  Savage of breed and of bone,
Shaggy and swift comes the yelping band
Freighters of fur from the voiceless land
  That sleeps in the Arctic zone.

Laden with skins from the north,
  Beaver and bear and raccoon,
Marten and mink from the polar belts,
Otter and ermine and sable pelts—
  The spoils of the hunter's moon.

Out of the night and the north,
  Sinewy, fearless and fleet,
Urging the pack through the pathless snow,
The Indian driver, calling low,
  Follows with moccasined feet.

Ships of the night and the north,
Freighters on prairies and plains,
Carrying cargoes from field and flood
They scent the trail through their wild red blood,
The wolfish blood in their veins.

"And He Said, Fight On"

Tennyson

Time and its ally, Dark Disarmament,
Have compassed me about,
Have massed their armies, and on battle bent
My forces put to rout;
But though I fight alone, and fall, and die,
Talk terms of Peace? Not I.

They war upon my fortress, and their guns
Are shattering its walls;
My army plays the cowards' part, and runs.
Pierced by a thousand balls;
They call for my surrender. I reply,
"Give quarter now? Not I."

They've shot my flag to ribbons, but in rents
It floats above the height;
Their ensign shall not crown my battlements
While I can stand and fight.
I fling defiance at them as I cry,
"Capitulate? Not I."

Frederick George Scott

Frederick George Scott was born on April 7, 1861 in Montréal, Québec. While many of our Confederation Poets were the sons or daughters of clergymen, Scott, a devoted Anglo-Catholic, became a clergyman himself, and served as such during the First World War, holding the rank of Major. Scott saw the horror of trench warfare up close, which he wrote about with great honesty, and his son was killed during the Battle of the Somme. Following the war, Scott held the post of Reverend Canon of St. Matthew's in Québec City, where he would die on January 19, 1944 while another world war raged.

Scott was, however, more than a war poet. He wrote many poems about the natural beauty of Canada, including some set in the Laurentians. As one might expect of an Anglican clergyman, God was never far from the poet's thoughts, and he found proof of God's glory and goodness in the natural wonders of his native Québec. Despite the savage brutality he experienced during the war, and the loss of his son in that conflict, his faith never faltered. Scott was the leading English-language poet in Québec during the Confederation Period.

The Temple of the Ages

These mountains sleep, white winter's mantle round them,
The thunder's voice no longer breaks their rest;
From bluest heights the sun beholds with rapture
The noble pose of each gigantic crest.

The generations of the clouds have vanished
Which lingered idly here through autumn days;
The leaves have gone, the voices of the tempest
No longer roll to heaven their hymn of praise.

Deep hid in snow, the streams with muffled murmurs
Pour down dark caverns to the infinite sea;
This awful peace has vexed their restless childhood;
They hurry from its dread solemnity.

Even the climbing woods are mute and spellbound,
And, halting midway on the steep ascent,
The patient spruces hold their breath for wonder,
Nor shake the snow with which their boughs are bent.

Now as the sun goes down with all his shining,
Huge shadows creep among these mighty walls,
And on the haunting ghosts of by-gone ages
The dreamy splendour of the starlight falls.

Not Nineveh, not Babylon nor Egypt,
In all their treasures 'neath the hungry sand,
Can show a sight so awful and majestic
As this waste temple in this newer land.

The king that reared these mighty courts was Chaos,
His servants, fire and elemental war;
The Titan hands of Earthquake and of Ocean
These granite slabs and pillars laid in store.

And, lauding here the vast and living Father,
The ages one by one have knelt and prayed,
Until the ghostly echoes of their worship
Come back and make man's puny heart afraid.

In the Winter Woods

Winter forests mutely standing
Naked on your bed of snow,
Wide your knotted arms expanding
To the biting winds that blow,
Nought ye heed of storm or stress,
Stubborn, silent, passionless.

Buried is each woodland treasure,
Gone the leaves and mossy rills,
Gone the birds that filled with pleasure
All the valleys and the hills;
Ye alone, a mighty host,
Stand like soldiers at your post.

Grim old trees, the words ye mutter,
Nodding in the frosty wind,
Waken thoughts I cannot utter,
But which haunt the heart and mind,
With a meaning, strange and deep,
As of visions seen in sleep.

Something in my inmost thinking
Tells me I am one with you,
For a subtle bond is linking
Nature's offspring through and through,
And your spirit like a flood
Stirs the pulses of my blood.

While I linger here and listen
　To the creaking boughs above,
Hung with icicles that glisten
　As if kindling into love,
Human heart and soul unite
With your majesty and might.

Horizontal, rich with glory,
　Through the boughs the red sun's rays
Clothe you as some grand life-story
　Robes an aged man with praise,
When, before his setting sun,
Men recount what he has done.

But the light is swiftly fading,
　And the wind is icy cold,
And a mist the moon is shading,
　Pallid in the western gold;
In the night-winds still ye nod,
Sentinels of Nature's God.

Now with laggard steps returning
　To the world from whence I came,
Leave I all the great West burning
　With the day that died in flame,
While the stars, with silver ray,
Light me on my homeward way.

The Unnamed Lake

It sleeps among the thousand hills
　Where no man ever trod,
And only nature's music fills
　The silences of God.

Great mountains tower above its shore,
 Green rushes fringe its brim,
And o'er its breast for evermore
 The wanton breezes skim.

Dark clouds that intercept the sun
 Go there in Spring to weep,
And there, when Autumn days are done,
 White mists lie down to sleep.

Sunrise and sunset crown with gold
 The peaks of ageless stone,
Where winds have thundered from of old
 And storms have set their throne.

No echoes of the world afar
 Disturb it night or day,
But sun and shadow, moon and star
 Pass and repass for aye.

'Twas in the grey of early dawn
 When first the lake we spied,
And fragments of a cloud were drawn
 Half down the mountain side.

Along the shore a heron flew,
 And from a speck on high
That hovered in the deepening blue,
 We heard the fish-hawk's cry.

Among the cloud-capt solitudes,
 No sound the silence broke,
Save when, in whispers down the woods,
 The guardian mountains spoke.

Through tangled brush and dewy brake,
Returning whence we came,
We passed in silence, and the lake
We left without a name.

My Friend Death

Will death come to me robed in black
With hollow eyes and toothless grin?
Will he have wings upon his back
And hold the scales to weigh my sin?
Shall I behold his face with dread
And strive to hide me from his sight,
When death sits down beside my bed
On my last night?

I picture death quite otherwise
Than such a spectre full of gloom,
As herald of the morning skies
To chase the darkness from my room,
An emanation from that star
Which lingers last above the dawn,
And sees the golden lands afar
And night withdrawn.

I like to think his voice is low
And filled with murmurs of the sea,
Where tides for ever ebb and flow
And taste the joys of destiny,
If death be such, when'er he come,
I shall lie tranquil to the end,
Then say, with lips to others dumb,
"I go, my friend."

Anniversary

The weary weeks come round again—
Come round again with frost and cold,
With falling leaves and dripping rain
And gleams of sun on autumn gold.

Through windows in the House of Time
I see great forces come and go,
I know the issues are sublime,
The trumpet-call to arms, I know.

But still my eyes go straining far,
Above the tumult and the noise,
To where, beyond the furthest star,
My darling plays among his toys.

I hear the laughter from his heart,
I see the sunshine in his eyes,
And then I waken with a start
And face once more the hollow skies.

By the Grave of Keats

The sunset gold was fading from the sky,
The cypresses towered darkly overhead,
While through the deepening shade a pathway led
To where the bones of England's poet lie.
We heard the night-wind in the tall trees sigh,
Yet, as we stooped and on the white stone read
Those lines which tell the heart's woe of the dead,
Something that was not darkness blurred the eye.

'Whose name was writ in water,'—yea, 'twas so.
O passionate soul of beauty, youth and light,
Thy name is writ in water, earth and air,
It sings in birds' songs, scents all flowers that blow,
Lights up the forest glade, crowns the starred night;
Thy epitaph was triumph, not despair.

The Mill-stream

Clear down the mountain, 'neath the arching green,
And o'er mossed boulders dappled by the sun,
With many a leap the laughing waters run.
They tumble fearless down each dark ravine,
And roam through caves where day has never been:
Until, at last, the open pool is won,
Where, by their prisoned strength, man's work is done
In that old mill which branching cedars screen.

Here, all day long, the massy logs, updrawn
Against the biting saw, are loud with shrieks.
Here, too, at night, are stars and mystery,
And nature sleeping; and, all round at dawn,
The rugged utterance of mountain peaks
Against the infinite silence of the sky.

Shakespeare

Unseen in the great minster dome of time,
Whose shafts are centuries, its spangled roof
The vaulted universe, our master sits,
And organ-voices like a far-off chime
Roll through the aisles of thought. The sunlight flits
From arch to arch, and, as he sits aloof,

Kings, heroes, priests, in concourse vast, sublime,
Whispers of love and cries from battle-field,
His wizard power breathes on the living air.

Warm faces gleam and pass, child, woman, man,
In the long multitude; but he, concealed,
Our bard eludes us, vainly each face we scan,
It is not he; his features are not there;
But, being thus hid, his greatness is revealed.

The Laurentians

These mountains reign alone, they do not share
The transitory life of woods and streams;
Wrapt in the deep solemnity of dreams,
They drain the sunshine of the upper air.
Beneath their peaks, the huge clouds, here and there,
Take counsel of the wind, which all night screams
Through grey, burnt forests where the moonlight beams
On hidden lakes, and rocks worn smooth and bare.

These mountains once, throned in the primal sea,
Shook half the world with thunder, and the sun
Pierced not the gloom that clung about their crest;
Now with spent force, toilers from toil set free,
Unvexed by fate, the part they played being done,
They watch and wait in venerable rest.

A Grave in Flanders

All night the tall trees overhead
Are whispering to the stars;
Their roots are wrapped about the dead
And hide the hideous scars.

The tide of war goes rolling by,
  The legions sweep along;
And daily in the summer sky
  The birds will sing their song.

No place is this for human tears,
  The time for tears is done;
Transfigured in these awful years,
  The two worlds blend in one.

This boy had visions while in life
  Of stars on distant skies,
So death came in the midst of strife
  A sudden, glad surprise.

He found the songs for which he yearned,
  Hopes that had mocked desire;
His heart is resting now, which burned
  With such consuming fire.

So down the ringing road we pass,
  And leave him where he fell.
The guardian trees, the waving grass,
  The birds will love him well.

St. Jans Capelle, 1915.

Quebec

Like some grey warder who, with mien sedate
  And smile of welcome, greets the throngs who pour
  Between the portals of a wide-thrown door,
Quebec stands guardian at our water gate,
And watches from her battlemented state

The great ships passing with their living store
Of human myriads coming to our shore,
Expectant, joyous, resolute, elate.
Behind her, voiceless to the frozen North,
The mountain wilderness unconquered lies;
Beneath her, rolls the river to the sea;
Upon her scroll of fame great names shine forth,
But on her storied crags from morning skies
There dawns the light of greater days to be.

Requiescant

In lonely watches night by night,
Great visions burst upon my sight,
For down the stretches of the sky
The hosts of dead go marching by.

Strange ghostly banners o'er them float,
Strange bugles sound an awful note,
And all their faces and their eyes
Are lit with starlight from the skies.

The anguish and the pain have passed
And peace hath come to them at last,
But in the stern looks linger still
The iron purpose and the will.

Dear Christ, who reign'st above the flood
Of human tears and human blood,
A weary road these men have trod,
O house them in the home of God.

In a field near Ypres.
April 1915.

Winter

I love the light in the golden eyes
Of the cottages up on the hill,
When the sun goes down at eventide,
And the fields are white and still;
The work of the winter's day is done,
The logs on the hearth-stone gleam,
While the children play at the close of day
And their elders sit and dream.

The stars, too, love the world at eve,
For they come out, one by one,
And look this way at the cottaged hill
And that at the buried sun.
And never the moan of a wind is heard
Through all the cloudless deep,
For the God above in his fatherly love
Has put the woods to sleep.

The Sea

O sea, thy voices spoke to me in childhood,
Wild and uncanny were the things they said,
When I have watched thy proud waves in the sunshine
Roll out along the beaches, white and dead.

They told me of the glory of blue stretches
Where wind and waves made music none might hear,
The mystery of ships and strange sea-monsters
And unknown lands across the hemisphere.

Now I have come to know a wider ocean—
Mysterious life and dreams and human pain;
While I and all things drift upon its bosom
To some dim shore whence no man comes again.

Out of the Storm

The huge winds gather on the midnight lake,
Shaggy with rain and loud with foam-white feet,
Then bound through miles of darkness till they meet
The harboured ships and city's squares, and wake
From steeples, domes and houses, sounds that take
A human speech, the storm's mad course to greet;
And nightmare voices through the rain and sleet
Pass shrieking, till the town's rock-sinews shake.

Howl, winds, around us in this silent room!
Wild lake, with thunders beat thy prison bars!
A brother's life is ebbing fast away,
And, mounting on your music through the gloom,
A pure soul mingles with the morning stars,
And with them melts into the blaze of day.

St. Luke's Hospital,
Duluth, May 17, 1894.

Last Post

On Vimy Ridge and Passchendaele,
Our silent armies sleep,
Through Summer's sun and Winter's gale
And 'neath the starry deep;
No more for them the dawn of day,
Nor sunset on the hill,
Their shouts and songs have died away,
Their giant strength is still.

The march of time goes swiftly by
And brings its care and toil,
But in eternal youth they lie
Beneath a foreign soil;
With iron limbs and fire for breath
They charged amidst the gloom,
And shared along those fields of death
The comradeship of doom.

Yet not in vain they watch and wait,
Strong champions of the right;
They are the sentries at our gate
And guard us through the night.
From selfish aim and paltry ease,
From slavery of the soul,
The men that save the land are these;
They point us to the goal.

Bliss Carman

The youngest of three first cousins, William Bliss Carman, like his older cousins—Barry Straton and Sir Charles G.D. Roberts—celebrated the spreading marshlands of the Bay of Fundy. Together, they helped imprint the grandeur of the Fundy region on the Canadian literary imagination. Carman was born on April 15, 1861 in Fredericton, New Brunswick. Like his older cousins, Carman attended the Fredericton Collegiate School, where he was influenced by Sir George Robert Parkin. His first book, *Low Tide on Grand Pré: A Book of Lyrics* (1893), established Carman as a major poet.

Carman moved to the United States where he studied at Harvard University. While in the U.S. he developed his unique version of Transcendentalism. He soon found a home in the American literary community, contributing to important anthologies like Jessie B. Rittenhouse's *The Younger American Poets* and Louis Untermeyer's *Modern American Poetry: A Critical Anthology.* Carman spent the last twenty-one years of his life in New Canaan, Connecticut, where he died on June 8, 1929. His body was returned to Fredericton, where he is buried.

A Windflower

Between the roadside and the wood,
    Between the dawning and the dew,
A tiny flower before the sun,
    Ephemeral in time, I grew.

And there upon the trail of spring,
    Not death nor love nor any name
Known among men in all their lands
    Could blur the wild desire with shame.

But down my dayspan of the year
    The feet of straying winds came by;
And all my trembling soul was thrilled
    To follow one lost mountain cry.

And then my heart beat once and broke
    To hear the sweeping rain forebode
Some ruin in the April world,
    Between the woodside and the road.

To-night can bring no healing now;
    The calm of yesternight is gone;
Surely the wind is but the wind,
    And I a broken waif thereon.

A Sea-Drift

As the seaweed swims the sea
    In the ruin after storm,
Sunburnt memories of thee
    Through the twilight float and form.

And desire, when thou art gone,
    Roves his desolate domain,
As the meadow-birds at dawn
    Haunt the spaces of the rain.

A Northern Vigil

Here by the gray north sea,
    In the wintry heart of the wild,
Comes the old dream of thee,
    Guendolen, mistress and child.

The heart of the forest grieves
    In the drift against my door;
A voice is under the eaves,
    A footfall on the floor.

Threshold, mirror and hall,
    Vacant and strangely aware,
Wait for their soul's recall
    With the dumb expectant air.

Here when the smouldering west
    Burns down into the sea,
I take no heed of rest
    And keep the watch for thee.

I sit by the fire and hear
    The restless wind go by,
On the long dirge and drear,
    Under the low bleak sky.

When day puts out to sea
And night makes in for land,
There is no lock for thee,
Each door awaits thy hand!

When night goes over the hill
And dawn comes down the dale,
It's O for the wild sweet will
That shall no more prevail!

When the zenith moon is round,
And snow-wraiths gather and run,
And there is set no bound
To love beneath the sun,

O wayward will, come near
The old mad willful way,
The soft mouth at my ear
With words too sweet to say!

Come, for the night is cold,
The ghostly moonlight fills
Hollow and rift and fold
Of the eerie Ardise hills!

The windows of my room
Are dark with bitter frost,
The stillness aches with doom
Of something loved and lost.

Outside, the great blue star
Burns in the ghostland pale,
Where giant Algebar
Holds on the endless trail.

Come, for the years are long,
And silence keeps the door,
Where shapes with the shadows throng
The firelit chamber floor.

Come, for thy kiss was warm,
With the red embers' glare
Across thy folding arm
And dark tumultuous hair!

And though thy coming rouse
The sleep-cry of no bird,
The keepers of the house
Shall tremble at thy word.

Come, for the soul is free!
In all the vast dreamland
There is no lock for thee,
Each door awaits thy hand.

Ah, not in dreams at all,
Fleering, perishing, dim,
But thy old self, supple and tall,
Mistress and child of whim!

The proud imperious guise,
Impetuous and serene,
The sad mysterious eyes,
And dignity of mien!

Yea, wilt thou not return,
When the late hill-winds veer,
And the bright hill-flowers burn
With the reviving year?

When April comes, and the sea
  Sparkles as if it smiled,
Will they restore to me
  My dark Love, empress and child?

The curtains seem to part;
  A sound is on the stair,
As if at the last . . . I start;
  Only the wind is there.

Lo, now far on the hills
  The crimson fumes uncurled,
Where the caldron mantles and spills
  Another dawn on the world!

The Eavesdropper

In a still room at hush of dawn,
  My Love and I lay side by side
And heard the roaming forest wind
  Stir in the paling autumn-tide.

I watched her earth-brown eyes grow glad
  Because the round day was so fair;
While memories of reluctant night
  Lurked in the blue dusk of her hair.

Outside, a yellow maple tree,
  Shifting upon the silvery blue
With tiny multitudinous sound,
  Rustled to let the sunlight through.

The livelong day the elvish leaves
    Danced with their shadows on the floor;
And the lost children of the wind
    Went straying homeward by our door.

And all the swarthy afternoon
    We watched the great deliberate sun
Walk through the crimsoned hazy world,
    Counting his hilltops one by one.

Then as the purple twilight came
    And touched the vines along our eaves,
Another Shadow stood without
    And gloomed the dancing of the leaves.

The silence fell on my Love's lips;
    Her great brown eyes were veiled and sad
With pondering some maze of dream,
    Though all the splendid year was glad.

Restless and vague as a gray wind
    Her heart had grown, she knew not why.
But hurrying to the open door,
    Against the verge of western sky

I saw retreating on the hills,
    Looming and sinister and black,
The stealthy figure swift and huge
    Of One who strode and looked not back.

The Vagabonds

"Such as wake on the night and sleep on the day, and haunt customable taverns and alehouses and routs about, and no man wot from whence they came, nor whither they go."—Old English Statute.

We are the vagabonds of time,
  And rove the yellow autumn days,
When all the roads are gray with rime
  And all the valleys blue with haze.

We came unlooked for as the wind
  Trooping across the April hills,
When the brown waking earth had dreams
  Of summer in the Wander Kills.

How far afield we joyed to fare,
  With June in every blade and tree!
Now with the sea-wind in our hair
  We turn our faces to the sea.

We go unheeded as the stream
  That wanders by the hill-wood side,
Till the great marshes take his hand
  And lead him to the roving tide.

The roving tide, the sleeping hills,
  These are the borders of that zone
Where they may fare as fancy wills
  Whom wisdom smiles and calls her own.

It is a country of the sun,
   Full of forgotten yesterdays,
When time takes Summer in his care,
   And fills the distance of her gaze.

It stretches from the open sea
   To the blue mountains and beyond;
The world is Vagabondia
   To him who is a vagabond.

In the beginning God made man
   Out of the wandering dust, men say;
And in the end his life shall be
   A wandering wind and blown away.

We are the vagabonds of time,
   Willing to let the world go by,
With joy supreme, with heart sublime,
   And valor in the kindling eye.

We have forgotten where we slept,
   And guess not where we sleep to-night,
Whether among the lonely hills
   In the pale streamers' ghostly light

We shall lie down and hear the frost
   Walk in the dead leaves restlessly,
Or somewhere on the iron coast
   Learn the oblivion of the sea.

It matters not. And yet I dream
   Of dreams fulfilled and rest somewhere
Before this restless heart is stilled
   And all its fancies blown to air.

Had I my will! . . . The sun burns down
   And something plucks my garment's hem;
The robins in their faded brown
   Would lure me to the south with them.

'Tis time for vagabonds to make
   The nearest inn. Far on I hear
The voices of the Northern hills
   Gather the vagrants of the year.

Brave heart, my soul! Let longings be!
   We have another day to wend.
For dark or waylay what care we
   Who have the lords of time to friend?

And if we tarry or make haste,
   The wayside sleep can hold no fear.
Shall fate unpoise, or whim perturb,
   The calm-begirt in dawn austere?

There is a tavern, I have heard,
   Not far, and frugal, kept by One
Who knows the children of the Word,
   And welcomes each when day is done.

Some say the house is lonely set
   In Northern night, and snowdrifts keep
The silent door; the hearth is cold,
   And all my fellows gone to sleep. . . .

Had I my will! I hear the sea
   Thunder a welcome on the shore;
I know where lies the hostelry
   And who should open me the door.

Legends of Lost Haven

There are legends of Lost Haven,
Come, I know not whence, to me,
When the wind is in the clover,
When the sun is on the sea.

There are rumors in the pine-tops,
There are whispers in the grass;
And the flocking crows at nightfall
Bring home hints of things that pass

Out upon the broad dike yonder,
All day long beneath the sun,
Where the tall ships cloud and settle
Down the sea-curve, one by one.

And the crickets in fine chorus—
Every slim and tiny reed—
Strive to chord the broken rhythmus
Of the world, and half succeed.

There are myriad traditions
Treasured by the talking rain;
And with memories the moonlight
Walks the cold and silent plain.

Where the river tells his hill-tales
To the lone complaining bar,
Where the midgets thread their dances
To the yellow twilight star,

Where the blossom bends to hearken
To the bee with velvet bands,
There are chronicles enciphered
Of the yet uncharted lands.

All the musical marauders
Of the berry and the bloom
Sing the lure of soul's illusion
Out of darkness, out of doom.

But the sure and great evangel
Comes when half alone I hear,
At the rosy door of silence,
Love, the lord of speech, draw near.

Then for once across the threshold,
Darkling spirit, thou art free,—
As thy hope is every ship makes
Some lost haven of the sea.

The Shadow Boatswain

Don't you know the sailing orders?
It is time to put to sea,
And the stranger in the harbor
Sends a boat ashore for me.

With the thunder of her canvas
Coming on the wind again,
I can hear the Shadow Boatswain
Piping to his shadow men.

Is it firelight or morning,
That red flicker on the floor?
Your good-by was braver, sweetheart,
When I sailed away before.

Think of this last lovely summer!
Love, what ails the wind to-night?
What's he saying in the chimney
Turns your berry cheek so white?

What a morning! How the sunlight
Sparkles on the outer bay,
Where the brig lies waiting for me
To trip anchor and away!

That's the Doomkeel. You may know her
By her clean run aft; and, then,
Don't you hear the Shadow Boatswain
Piping to his shadow men?

Off the freshening sea to windward,
Is it a white tern I hear
Shrilling in the gusty weather
Where the far sea-line is clear?

What a morning for departure!
How your blue eyes melt and shine!
Will you watch us from the headland
Till we sink below the line?

I can see the wind already
Steer the scurf marks of the tide,
As we slip the wake of being
Down the sloping world and wide.

I can feel the vasty mountains
Heave and settle under me,
And the Doomkeel veer and shudder,
Crumbling on the hollow sea.

There's a call, as when a white gull
Cries and beats across the blue;
That must be the Shadow Boatswain
Piping to his shadow crew.

There's a boding sound, like winter
When the pines begin to quail;
That must be the gray wind moaning
In the belly of the sail.

I can feel the icy fingers
Creeping in upon my bones;
There must be a berg to windward
Somewhere in these border zones.

Stir the fire.... I love the sunlight,—
Always loved my shipmate sun.
How the sunflowers beckon to me
From the dooryard one by one!

How the royal lady roses
Strew this summer world of ours!
There'll be none in Lonely Haven;
It is too far north for flowers.

There, sweetheart! And I must leave you.
What should touch my wife with tears?
There's no danger with the Master;
He has sailed the sea for years.

With the sea-wolves on her quarter,
And a white bone in her teeth,
He will steer the shadow cruiser,
Dark before and doom beneath,

Down the last expanse, till morning
Flares above the broken sea,
And the midnight storm is over,
And the Isles are close alee.

So some twilight, when your roses
Are all blown and it is June,
You will turn your blue eyes seaward
Through the white dusk of the moon,

Wondering, as that far sea-cry
Comes upon the wind again,
And you hear the Shadow Boatswain
Piping to his shadow men.

The Ships of Saint John

Where are the ships I used to know,
　　That came to port on the Fundy tide
Half a century ago,
　　In beauty and stately pride?

In they would come past the beacon light,
　　With the sun on gleaming sail and spar,
Folding their wings like birds in flight
　　From countries strange and far.

Schooner and brig and barkentine,
　　I watched them slow as the sails were furled,
And wondered what cities they must have seen
　　On the other side of the world.

Frenchman and Britisher and Dane,
　　Yankee, Spaniard and Portugee,
And many a home ship back again
　　With her stories of the sea.

Calm and victorious, at rest
  From the relentless, rough sea-play,
The wild duck on the river's breast
  Was not more sure than they.

The creatures of a passing race,
  The dark spruce forests made them strong,
The sea's lore gave them magic grace,
  The great winds taught them song.

And God endowed them each with life—
  His blessing on the craftsman's skill—
To meet the blind unreasoned strife
  And dare the risk of ill.

Not mere insensate wood and paint
  Obedient to the helm's command,
But often restive as a saint
  Beneath the Heavenly hand.

All the beauty and mystery
  Of life were there, adventure bold,
Youth, and the glamour of the sea
  And all its sorrows old.

And many a time I saw them go
  Out on the flood at morning brave,
As the little tugs had them in tow,
  And the sunlight danced on the wave.

There all day long you could hear the sound
  Of the caulking iron, the ship's bronze bell,
And the clank of the capstan going round
  As the great tides rose and fell.

The sailors' songs, the Captain's shout,
The boatswain's whistle piping shrill,
And the roar as the anchor chain runs out,—
I often hear them still.

I can see them still, the sun on their gear,
The shining streak as the hulls careen,
And the flag at the peak unfurling,—clear
As a picture on a screen.

The fog still hangs on the long tide-rips,
The gulls go wavering to and fro,
But where are all the beautiful ships
I knew so long ago?

The Cry of the Hillborn

I am homesick for the mountains—
My heroic mother hills—
And the longing that is on me
No solace ever stills.

I would climb to brooding summits
With their old untarnished dreams,
Cool my heart in forest shadows
To the lull of falling streams;

Hear the innocence of aspens
That babble in the breeze,
And the fragrant sudden showers
That patter on the trees.

I am lonely for my thrushes
In their hermitage withdrawn,
Toning the quiet transports
Of twilight and of dawn.

I need the pure, strong mornings,
When the soul of day is still,
With the touch of frost that kindles
The scarlet on the hill;

Lone trails and winding woodroads
To outlooks wild and high,
And the pale moon waiting sundown
Where ledges cut the sky.

I dream of upland clearings
Where cones of sumac burn,
And gaunt and gray-mossed boulders
Lie deep in beds of fern;

The gray and mottled beeches,
The birches' satin sheen,
The majesty of hemlocks
Crowning the blue ravine.

My eyes dim for the skyline
Where purple peaks aspire,
And the forges of the sunset
Flare up in golden fire.

There crests look down unheeding
And see the great winds blow,
Tossing the huddled tree-tops
In gorges far below;

Where cloud-mists from the warm earth
Roll up about their knees,
And hang their filmy tatters
Like prayers upon the trees.

I cry for night-blue shadows
On plain and hill and dome,—
The spell of old enchantments,
The sorcery of home.

Fireflies

The fireflies across the dusk
Are flashing signals through the gloom—
Courageous messengers of light
That dare immensities of doom.

About the seeding meadow-grass,
Like busy watchmen in the street,
They come and go, they turn and pass,
Lighting the way for Beauty's feet.

Or up they float on viewless wings
To twinkle high among the trees,
And rival with soft glimmerings
The shining of the Pleiades.

The stars that wheel above the hill
Are not more wonderful to see,
Nor the great tasks that they fulfill
More needed in eternity.

In October

Now come the rosy dogwoods,
The golden tulip-tree,
And the scarlet yellow maple,
To make a day for me.

The ash-trees on the ridges,
The alders in the swamp,
Put on their red and purple
To join the autumn pomp.

The woodbine hangs her crimson
Along the pasture wall,
And all the bannered sumacs
Have heard the frosty call.

Who then so dead to valor
As not to raise a cheer,
When all the woods are marching
In triumph of the year?

The Ghost-yard of the Goldenrod

When the first silent frost has trod
The ghost-yard of the goldenrod,

And laid the blight of his cold hand
Upon the warm autumnal land,

And all things wait the subtle change
That men call death, is it not strange

That I—without a care or need,
Who only am an idle weed—

Should wait unmoved, so frail, so bold,
The coming of the final cold!

Winter Twilight

Along the wintry skyline,
Crowning the rocky crest,
Stands the bare screen of hardwood trees
Against the saffron west,—
Its gray and purple network
Of branching tracery
Outspread upon the lucent air,
Like weed within the sea.

The scarlet robe of autumn
Renounced and put away,
The mystic Earth is fairer still,—
A Puritan in gray.
The spirit of the winter,
How tender, how austere!
Yet all the ardor of the spring
And summer's dream are here.

Fear not, O timid lover,
The touch of frost and rime!
This is the virtue that sustained
The roses in their prime.
The anthem of the northwind
Shall hallow thy despair,
The benediction of the snow
Be answer to thy prayer.

And now the star of evening
That is the pilgrim's sign,
Is lighted in the primrose dusk,—
A lamp before a shrine.
Peace fills the mighty minster,
Tranquil and gray and old,
And all the chancel of the west
Is bright with paling gold.

A little wind goes sifting
Along the meadow floor,—
Like steps of lovely penitents
Who sighingly adore.
Then falls the twilight curtain,
And fades the eerie light,
And frost and silence turn the keys
In the great doors of night.

Archibald Lampman

The son of a clergyman, like so many of the other Confederation Poets, and raised in the church, Archibald Lampman was born on November 17, 1861 in Morpeth, Ontario. He attended Trinity College, University of Toronto, and eventually moved to Ottawa for a government job. There he met Duncan Campbell Scott and Wilfred Campbell, and together they wrote a column for *The Globe* called "At The Mermaid Inn." Lampman and Scott took several long canoe trips into northern Ontario, and both wrote excellent poems about the Canadian Shield. Indeed, Lampman's poetry of the North is among his greatest contributions to our literature.

Lampman died young on February 10, 1899 at Ottawa, Ontario. He was only able to assemble three volumes of poetry, but did not live to see the third in print. As a result, much, if not most, of his best work was not published until a year after his death. At that time Duncan Campbell Scott edited *The Poems of Archibald Lampman*, and the poet's reputation was firmly established. Lampman was like Crawford and Cameron, two poets who also had to wait until death to be seen by critics and general readers as truly major poets. And although Lampman did not reach the twentieth century, in poems like "The City of the End of Things" he was able to see that the future was not necessarily going to be all that nice, that the romantic dream of Canada, so common during the decades following Confederation, might actually fail. To the present day, he remains the foremost poet of his era.

Heat

From plains that reel to southward, dim,
The road runs by me white and bare;
Up the steep hill it seems to swim
Beyond, and melt into the glare.
Upward half way, or it may be
Nearer the summit, slowly steals
A hay-cart, moving dustily
With idly clacking wheels.

By his cart's side the wagoner
Is slouching slowly at his ease,
Half-hidden in the windless blur
Of white dust puffing to his knees.
This wagon on the height above,
From sky to sky on either hand,
Is the sole thing that seems to move
In all the heat-held land.

Beyond me in the fields the sun
Soaks in the grass and hath his will;
I count the marguerites one by one;
Even the buttercups are still.
On the brook yonder not a breath
Disturbs the spider or the midge.
The water-bugs draw close beneath
The cool gloom of the bridge.

Where the far elm-tree shadows flood
Dark patches in the burning grass,
The cows, each with her peaceful cud,
Lie waiting for the heat to pass.
From somewhere on the slope near by
Into the pale depth of the noon
A wandering thrush slides leisurely
His thin revolving tune.

In intervals of dreams I hear
    The cricket from the droughty ground;
The grass-hoppers spin into mine ear
    A small innumerable sound.
I lift mine eyes sometimes to gaze:
    The burning sky-line blinds my sight:
The woods far off are blue with haze:
    The hills are drenched in light.

And yet to me not this or that
    Is always sharp or always sweet;
In the sloped shadow of my hat
    I lean at rest, and drain the heat;
Nay more, I think some blessèd power
    Hath brought me wandering idly here:
In the full furnace of this hour
    My thoughts grow keen and clear.

Among the Timothy

Long hours ago, while yet the morn was blithe,
    Nor sharp athirst had drunk the beaded dew,
A reaper came, and swung his cradled scythe
    Around this stump, and, shearing slowly, drew
    Far round among the clover, ripe for hay,
        A circle clean and grey;
And here among the scented swathes that gleam,
    Mixed with dead daisies, it is sweet to lie
    And watch the grass and the few-clouded sky,
        Nor think but only dream.

For when the noon was turning, and the heat
Fell down most heavily on field and wood,
I too came hither, borne on restless feet,
Seeking some comfort for an aching mood.
Ah, I was weary of the drifting hours,
The echoing city towers,
The blind grey streets, the jingle of the throng,
Weary of hope that like a shape of stone
Sat near at hand without a smile or moan,
And weary most of song.

And those high moods of mine that sometime made
My heart a heaven, opening like a flower,
A sweeter world where I in wonder strayed,
Begirt with shapes of beauty and the power
Of dreams that moved through that enchanted clime
With changing breaths of rhyme,
Were all gone lifeless now like those white leaves,
That hang all winter, shivering dead and blind
Among the sinewy beeches in the wind,
That vainly calls and grieves.

Ah! I will set no more mine overtaskèd brain
To barren search and toil that beareth nought,
Forever following with sorefooted pain
The crossing pathways of unbournèd thought;
But let it go, as one that hath no skill,
To take what shape it will,
An ant slow-burrowing in the earthy gloom,
A spider bathing in the dew at morn,
Or a brown bee in wayward fancy borne
From hidden bloom to bloom.

Hither and thither o'er the rocking grass
The little breezes, blithe as they are blind,
Teasing the slender blossoms pass and pass,
Soft-footed children of the gipsy wind,
To taste of every purple-fringèd head
Before the bloom is dead;
And scarcely heed the daisies that, endowed
With stems so short they cannot see, up-bear
Their innocent sweet eyes distressed, and stare
Like children in a crowd.

Not far to fieldward in the central heat,
Shadowing the clover, a pale poplar stands
With glimmering leaves that, when the wind comes, beat
Together like innumerable small hands,
And with the calm, as in vague dreams astray,
Hang wan and silver-grey;
Like sleepy mænads, who in pale surprise,
Half-wakened by a prowling beast, have crept
Out of the hidden covert, where they slept,
At noon with languid eyes.

The crickets creak, and through the noonday glow,
That crazy fiddler of the hot mid-year,
The dry cicada plies his wiry bow
In long-spun cadence, thin and dusty sere:
From the green grass the small grasshoppers' din
Spreads soft and silvery thin:
And ever and anon a murmur steals
Into mine ears of toil that moves alway,
The crackling rustle of the pitch-forked hay
And lazy jerk of wheels.

As so I lie and feel the soft hours wane,
To wind and sun and peaceful sound laid bare,
That aching dim discomfort of the brain
Fades off unseen, and shadowy-footed care
Into some hidden corner creeps at last
To slumber deep and fast;
And gliding on, quite fashioned to forget,
From dream to dream I bid my spirit pass
Out into the pale green ever-swaying grass
To brood, but no more fret.

And hour by hour among all shapes that grow
Of purple mints and daisies gemmed with gold
In sweet unrest my visions come and go;
I feel and hear and with quiet eyes behold;
And hour by hour, the ever-journeying sun,
In gold and shadow spun,
Into mine eyes and blood, and through the dim
Green glimmering forest of the grass shines down,
Till flower and blade, and every cranny brown,
And I are soaked with him.

In October

Along the waste, a great way off, the pines,
Like tall slim priests of storm, stand up and bar
The low long strip of dolorous red that lines
The under west, where wet winds moan afar.
The cornfields all are brown, and brown the meadows
With the blown leaves' wind-heapèd traceries,
And the brown thistle stems that cast no shadows,
And bear no bloom for bees.

As slowly earthward leaf by red leaf slips,
The sad trees rustle in chill misery,
A soft strange inner sound of pain-crazed lips,
That move and murmur incoherently;
As if all leaves, that yet have breath, were sighing,
With pale hushed throats, for death is at the door,
So many low soft masses for the dying
Sweet leaves that live no more.

Here I will sit upon this naked stone,
Draw my coat closer with my numbèd hands,
And hear the ferns sigh, and the wet woods moan,
And send my heart out to the ashen lands;
And I will ask myself what golden madness,
What balmèd breaths of dreamland spicery,
What visions of soft laughter and light sadness
Were sweet last month to me.

The dry dead leaves flit by with thin weird tunes,
Like failing murmurs of some conquered creed,
Graven in mystic markings with strange runes,
That none but stars and biting winds may read;
Here I will wait a little; I am weary,
Not torn with pain of any lurid hue,
But only still and very gray and dreary,
Sweet sombre lands, like you.

Solitude

How still it is here in the woods. The trees
Stand motionless, as if they did not dare
To stir, lest it should break the spell. The air
Hangs quiet as spaces in a marble frieze.
Even this little brook, that runs at ease,
Whispering and gurgling in its knotted bed,
Seems but to deepen with its curling thread
Of sound the shadowy sun-pierced silences.

Sometimes a hawk screams or a woodpecker
Startles the stillness from its fixèd mood
With his loud careless tap. Sometimes I hear
The dreamy white-throat from some far off tree
Pipe slowly on the listening solitude
His five pure notes succeeding pensively.

At the Ferry

On such a day the shrunken stream
Spends its last water and runs dry;
Clouds like far turrets in a dream
Stand baseless in the burning sky.
On such a day at every rod
The toilers in the hay-field halt,
With dripping brows, and the parched sod
Yields to the crushing foot like salt.

But here a little wind astir,
Seen waterward in jetting lines,
From yonder hillside topped with fir
Comes pungent with the breath of pines;
And here when all the noon hangs still,
White-hot upon the city tiles,
A perfume and a wintry chill
Breathe from the yellow lumber-piles.

And all day long there falls a blur
Of noises upon listless ears,
The rumble of the trams, the stir
Of barges at the clacking piers;
The champ of wheels, the crash of steam,
And ever, without change or stay,
The drone, as through a troubled dream,
Of waters falling far away.

A tug-boat up the farther shore
   Half pants, half whistles, in her draught;
The cadence of a creaking oar
   Falls drowsily; a corded raft
Creeps slowly in the noonday gleam,
   And wheresoe'er a shadow sleeps
The men lie by, or half a-dream,
   Stand leaning at the idle sweeps.

And all day long in the quiet bay
   The eddying amber depths retard,
And hold, as in a ring, at play,
   The heavy saw-logs notched and scarred;
And yonder between cape and shoal,
   Where the long currents swing and shift,
An aged punt-man with his pole
   Is searching in the parted drift.

At moments from the distant glare
   The murmur of a railway steals
Round yonder jutting point the air
   Is beaten with the puff of wheels;
And here at hand an open mill,
   Strong clamor at perpetual drive,
With changing chant, now hoarse, now shrill,
   Keeps dinning like a mighty hive.

A furnace over field and mead,
   The rounding noon hangs hard and white;
Into the gathering heats recede
   The hollows of the Chelsea height;
But under all to one quiet tune,
   A spirit in cool depths withdrawn,
With logs, and dust, and wrack bestrewn,
   The stately river journeys on.

I watch the swinging currents go
   Far down to where, enclosed and piled,
The logs crowd, and the Gatineau
   Comes rushing from the northern wild.
I see the long low point, where close
   The shore-lines, and the waters end,
I watch the barges pass in rows
   That vanish at the tapering bend.

I see as at the noon's pale core—
   A shadow that lifts clear and floats—
The cabin'd village round the shore,
   The landing and the fringe of boats;
Faint films of smoke that curl and wreathe,
   And upward with the like desire
The vast gray church that seems to breathe
   In heaven with its dreaming spire.

And there the last blue boundaries rise,
   That guard within their compass furled
This plot of earth: beyond them lies
   The mystery of the echoing world;
And still my thought goes on, and yields
   New vision and new joy to me,
Far peopled hills, and ancient fields,
   And cities by the crested sea.

I see no more the barges pass,
   Nor mark the ripple round the pier,
And all the uproar, mass on mass,
   Falls dead upon a vacant ear.
Beyond the tumult of the mills,
   And all the city's sound and strife,
Beyond the waste, beyond the hills,
   I look far out and dream of life.

September

Now hath the summer reached her golden close,
   And, lost amid her corn-fields, bright of soul,
Scarcely perceives from her divine repose
   How near, how swift, the inevitable goal:
Still, still, she smiles, though from her careless feet
   The bounty and the fruitful strength are gone,
   And through the soft long wondering days goes on
The silent sere decadence sad and sweet.

The kingbird and the pensive thrush are fled,
   Children of light, too fearful of the gloom;
The sun falls low, the secret word is said,
   The mouldering woods grow silent as the tomb;
Even the fields have lost their sovereign grace,
   The cone-flower and the marguerite; and no more,
   Across the river's shadow-haunted floor,
The paths of skimming swallows interlace.

Already in the outland wilderness
   The forests echo with unwonted dins;
In clamorous gangs the gathering woodmen press
   Northward, and the stern winter's toil begins.
Around the long low shanties, whose rough lines
   Break the sealed dreams of many an unnamed lake,
   Already in the frost-clear morns awake
The crash and thunder of the falling pines.

Where the tilled earth, with all its fields set free,
   Naked and yellow from the harvest lies,
By many a loft and busy granary,
   The hum and tumult of the thrashers rise;
There the tanned farmers labor without slack,
   Till twilight deepens round the spouting mill,
   Feeding the loosened sheaves, or with fierce will,
Pitching waist-deep upon the dusty stack.

Still a brief while, ere the old year quite pass,
Our wandering steps and wistful eyes shall greet
The leaf, the water, the beloved grass;
Still from these haunts and this accustomed seat
I see the wood-wrapt city, swept with light,
The blue long-shadowed distance, and, between,
The dotted farm-lands with their parcelled green,
The dark pine forest and the watchful height.

I see the broad rough meadow stretched away
Into the crystal sunshine, wastes of sod,
Acres of withered vervain, purple-gray,
Branches of aster, groves of goldenrod;
And yonder, toward the sunlit summit, strewn
With shadowy boulders, crowned and swathed with weed,
Stand ranks of silken thistles, blown to seed,
Long silver fleeces shining like the noon.

In far-off russet corn-fields, where the dry
Gray shocks stand peaked and withering, half concealed
In the rough earth, the orange pumpkins lie,
Full-ribbed; and in the windless pasture-field
The sleek red horses o'er the sun-warmed ground
Stand pensively about in companies,
While all around them from the motionless trees
The long clean shadows sleep without a sound.

Under cool elm-trees floats the distant stream,
Moveless as air; and o'er the vast warm earth
The fathomless daylight seems to stand and dream,
A liquid cool elixir—all its girth
Bound with faint haze, a frail transparency,
Whose lucid purple barely veils and fills
The utmost valleys and the thin last hills,
Nor mars one whit their perfect clarity.

Thus without grief the golden days go by,
So soft we scarcely notice how they wend,
And like a smile half happy, or a sigh,
The summer passes to her quiet end;
And soon, too soon, around the cumbered eaves
Sly frosts shall take the creepers by surprise,
And through the wind-touched reddening woods shall rise
October with the rain of ruined leaves.

An Autumn Landscape

No wind there is that either pipes or moans;
The fields are cold and still; the sky
Is covered with a blue-gray sheet
Of motionless cloud; and at my feet
The river, curling softly by,
Whispers and dimples round its quiet gray stones.

Along the chill green slope that dips and heaves
The road runs rough and silent, lined
With plum-trees, misty and blue-gray,
And poplars pallid as the day,
In masses spectral, undefined,
Pale greenish stems half hid in dry gray leaves.

And on beside the river's sober edge
A long fresh field lies black. Beyond,
Low thickets gray and reddish stand,
Stroked white with birch; and near at hand,
Over a little steel-smooth pond,
Hang multitudes of thin and withering sedge.

Across a waste and solitary rise
A ploughman urges his dull team,
A stooped gray figure with prone brow
That plunges bending to the plough
With strong, uneven steps. The stream
Rings and re-echoes with his furious cries.

Sometimes the lowing of a cow, long-drawn,
Comes from far off; and crows in strings
Pass on the upper silences.
A flock of small gray goldfinches,
Flown down with silvery twitterings,
Rustle among the birch-cones and are gone.

This day the season seems like one that heeds,
With fixèd ear and lifted hand,
All moods that yet are known on earth,
All motions that have faintest birth,
If haply she may understand
The utmost inward sense of all her deeds.

Voices of Earth

We have not heard the music of the spheres,
The song of star to star, but there are sounds
More deep than human joy and human tears,
That Nature uses in her common rounds;
The fall of streams, the cry of winds that strain
The oak, the roaring of the sea's surge, might
Of thunder breaking afar off, or rain
That falls by minutes in the summer night.
These are the voices of earth's secret soul,
Uttering the mystery from which she came.
To him who hears them grief beyond control,

Or joy inscrutable without a name,
Wakes in his heart thoughts bedded there, impearled,
Before the birth and making of the world.

Winter Evening

To-night the very horses springing by
Toss gold from whitened nostrils. In a dream
The streets that narrow to the westward gleam
Like rows of golden palaces; and high
From all the crowded chimneys tower and die
A thousand aureoles. Down in the west
The brimming plains beneath the sunset rest,
One burning sea of gold. Soon, soon shall fly
The glorious vision, and the hours shall feel
A mightier master; soon from height to height,
With silence and the sharp unpitying stars,
Stern creeping frosts, and winds that touch like steel,
Out of the depth beyond the eastern bars,
Glittering and still shall come the awful night.

Beauty

Only the things of Beauty shall endure.
While man goes woeful, wasting his brief day,
From Truth and Love and Nature far astray,
Lo! Beauty, the lost goal, the unsought cure;
For how can he whom Beauty hath made sure,
Who hath her law and sovereign creed by heart,
Be proud, or pitiless, play the tyrant's part,
Be false, or envious, greedy or impure.
Nay! she will gift him with a golden key
To unlock every virtue. Name not ye,

As once, "the good, the beautiful, the true,"
For these are but three names for one sole thing;
Or rather Beauty is the perfect ring
That circles and includes the other two.

At Dusk

Already o'er the west the first star shines,
And day and dark are imperceptibly linked;
The fences and pied fields grow indistinct,
Deep beyond deep the living light declines,
Still lingering o'er the westward mountain lines,
Pallid and clear; and on its silent breast
A symbol of eternal quiet rest,
Far and black-plumed, the imperturbable pines.
A few thin threads of purple clouds still float
In the serene ether, and the night wind,
Wandering in puffs from off the darkening hill,
Breathes warm or cool; and now the whip-poor-will,
Beyond the river margins glassed and thinned,
Whips the cool hollows with his liquid note.

A Sunset at Les Eboulements

Broad shadows fall. On all the mountain side
The scythe-swept fields are silent. Slowly home
By the long beach the high-piled hay-carts come,
Splashing the pale salt shallows. Over wide
Fawn-coloured wastes of mud the slipping tide,
Round the dun rocks and wattled fisheries,
Creeps murmuring in. And now by twos and threes,
O'er the slow spreading pools with clamorous chide,
Belated crows from strip to strip take flight.

Soon will the first star shine; yet ere the night
Reach onward to the pale-green distances,
The sun's last shaft beyond the gray sea-floor
Still dreams upon the Kamouraska shore,
And the long line of golden villages.

To a Millionaire

The world in gloom and splendour passes by,
And thou in the midst of it with brows that gleam,
A creature of that old distorted dream
That makes the sound of life an evil cry.
Good men perform just deeds, and brave men die,
And win not honour such as gold can give,
While the vain multitudes plod on, and live,
And serve the curse that pins them down: But I
Think only of the unnumbered broken hearts,
The hunger and the mortal strife for bread,
Old age and youth alike mistaught, misfed,
By want and rags and homelessness made vile,
The griefs and hates, and all the meaner parts
That balance thy one grim misgotten pile.

The Modern Politician

What manner of soul is his to whom high truth
Is but the plaything of a feverish hour,
A dangling ladder to the ghost of power!
Gone are the grandeurs of the world's iron youth,
When kings were mighty, being made by swords.
Now comes the transit age, the age of brass,
When clowns into the vacant empires pass,
Blinding the multitude with specious words.

To them faith, kinship, truth and verity,
Man's sacred rights and very holiest thing,
Are but the counters at a desperate play,
Flippant and reckless what the end may be,
So that they glitter, each his little day,
The little mimic of a vanished king.

A January Morning

The glittering roofs are still with frost; each worn
Black chimney builds into the quiet sky
Its curling pile to crumble silently.
Far out to westward on the edge of morn,
The slender misty city towers up-borne
Glimmer faint rose against the pallid blue;
And yonder on those northern hills, the hue
Of amethyst, hang fleeces dull as horn.
And here behind me come the woodmen's sleighs
With shouts and clamorous squeakings; might and main
Up the steep slope the horses stamp and strain,
Urged on by hoarse-tongued drivers—cheeks ablaze,
Iced beards and frozen eyelids—team by team,
With frost-fringed flanks, and nostrils jetting steam.

A Forest Path in Winter

Along this secret and forgotten road
    All depths and forest forms, above, below,
    Are plumed and draped and hillocked with the snow.
A branch cracks now and then, and its soft load
Drifts by me in a thin prismatic shower;
    Else not a sound, but vistas bound and crossed
    With sheeted gleams and sharp blue shadows, frost,

And utter silence. In his glittering power
The master of mid-winter reveries
    Holds all things buried soft and strong and deep.
    The busy squirrel has his hidden lair;
And even the spirits of the stalwart trees
    Have crept into their utmost roots, and there,
Upcoiled in the close earth, lie fast asleep.

After Mist

Last night there was a mist. Pallid and chill
The yellow moon-blue clove the thickening sky,
And all night long a gradual wind crept by,
And froze the fog, and with minutest skill
Fringed it and forked it, adding bead to bead,
In spears, and feathery tufts, and delicate hems
Round windward trunks, and all the topmost stems,
And every bush, and every golden weed;
And now upon the meadows silvered through
And forests frosted to their farthest pines—
A last faint gleam upon the misty blue—
The magic of the morning falls and shines,
A creamy splendour on a dim white world,
Broidered with violet, crystalled and impearled.

In Beechwood Cemetery

Here the dead sleep—the quiet dead. No sound
Disturbs them ever, and no storm dismays.
Winter mid snow caresses the tired ground,
And the wind roars about the woodland ways.
Springtime and summer and red autumn pass,
With leaf and bloom and pipe of wind and bird,

And the old earth puts forth her tender grass,
By them unfelt, unheeded and unheard.
Our centuries to them are but as strokes
In the dim gamut of some far-off chime.
Unaltering rest their perfect being cloaks—
A thing too vast to hear or feel or see—
Children of Silence and Eternity,
They know no season but the end of time.

Goldenrod

Ere the stout year be waxed shrewd and old,
And while the grain upon the well-piled stack
Waits yet unthreshed, by every woodland track,
Low stream, and meadow, and wide waste outrolled,
By every fence that skirts the forest mould,
Sudden and thick, as at the reaper's hail,
They come, companions of the harvest, frail
Green forests yellowing upward into gold.
Lo, where yon shaft of level sunshine gleams
Full on those pendent wreathes, those bounteous plumes
So gracious and so golden! Mark them well,
The last and best from summer's empty looms,
Her benedicite, and dream of dreams,
The fulness of her soul made visible.

On Lake Temiscamingue

A single dreamy elm, that stands between
    The sombre forest and the wan-lit lake,
Halves with its slim gray stem and pendent green
    The shadowed point. Beyond it without break
Bold brows of pine-topped granite bend away,

Far to the southward, fading off in grand
Soft folds of looming purple. Cool and gray,
The point runs out, a blade of thinnest sand.
Two rivers meet beyond it: wild and clear,
Their deepening thunder breaks upon the ear—
The one descending from its forest home
By many an eddied pool and murmuring fall—
The other cloven through the mountain wall,
A race of tumbled rocks, a roar of foam.

Night in the Wilderness

The good fire-ranger is our friend to-night;
We sit before his tent, and watch his fire
Send up its fount of sailing sparks that light
The ruddy pine-stems. Hands that never tire
Our friend's are, as he spreads his frugal store,
And cooks his bouillon with a hunter's pride,
Till, warm with woodland fare and forest lore
We sink at last to sleep. On every side,
A grim mysterious presence, vast and old,
The forest stretches leagues on leagues away,
With lonely rivers running dark and cold,
And many a gloomy lake and haunted bay.
The stars above the pines are sharp and still.
The wind scarce moves. An owl hoots from the hill.

In the Wilds

We run with rushing streams that toss and spume;
We speed or dream upon the open meres;
The pine-woods fold us in their pungent gloom;
The thunder of wild water fills our ears;

The rain we take, we take the beating sun;
The stars are cold above our heads at night;
On the rough earth we lie when day is done,
And slumber even in the storm's despite.
The savage vigour of the forest creeps
Into our veins, and laughs upon our lips;
The warm blood kindles from forgotten deeps,
And surges tingling to the finger tips.
The deep-pent life awakes and bursts its bands;
We feel the strength and goodness of our hands.

To the Ottawa

Dear dark-brown waters full of all the stain
Of sombre spruce-woods and the forest fens,
Laden with sound from far-off northern glens
Where winds and craggy cataracts complain,
Voices of streams and mountain pines astrain,
The pines that brood above the roaring foam
Of La Montagne or Des Erables; thine home
Is distant yet, a shelter far to gain.
Aye still to eastward, past the shadowy lake
And the long slopes of Rigaud toward the sun,
The mightier stream, thy comrade, waits for thee,
The beryl waters that espouse and take
Thine in their deep embrace, and bear thee on
In that great bridal journey to the sea.

Winter Uplands

The frost that stings like fire upon my cheek,
The loneliness of this forsaken ground,
The long white drift upon whose powered peak

I sit in the great silence as one bound;
The rippled sheet of snow where the wind blew
Across the open fields for miles ahead;
The far-off city towered and roofed in blue
A tender line upon the western red;
The stars that singly, then in flocks appear,
Like jets of silver from the violet dome,
So wonderful, so many and so near,
And then the golden moon to light me home—
The crunching snowshoes and the stinging air,
And silence, frost and beauty everywhere.

Duncan Campbell Scott

No poet of the Confederation Period, or since, has done more to establish the seminal importance of the North than Duncan Campbell Scott. Scott believed that Canada had a spirit, and perhaps a *meaning*, and that this could best be discovered deep in the vast Canadian Shield, especially the land between Lake Superior and James Bay. He wrote about this in poems like "The Height of Land." Somehow, the austere beauty of the wilderness spoke directly about the very nature of Canada. Our poet was born on August 2, 1862 in Ottawa, Ontario. His employment as a treaty negotiator for the Department of Indian Affairs led him to travel extensively throughout northern Ontario, and this influenced his views of the Indigenous tribes living in the area. Importantly, he introduced his friend, Archibald Lampman, to the Canadian Shield. This led directly to Lampman's northern poems such as "Temagami," "On Lake Temiscamingue," and "In the Wilds," which are among his most important works.

Scott's poetry also examined the conflict between European settlers and the Indigenous Peoples. This is most notable in his poems like "On the Way to the Mission." As the critic Gordon Johnston wrote in *Duncan Campbell Scott and His Works*, "his attempt to see the Indians as themselves, and not as merely decorative or illustrative," marked "the beginning of an extensive interest in the natives in later poets." It must be noted that Scott's relationship with Canada's Indigenous communities was deeply conflicted and complex, and today is highly controversial. Especially concerning were Scott's role with the infamous Residential Schools (schools that were most often administered by the Catholic Church, and considered by Pope

Francis to have been genocidal), and that he served as the chief federal negotiator for Treaty No. 9 in 1905. Following a long and productive life, Scott died on December 19, 1947 at Ottawa, Ontario.

Rapids at Night

Here at the roots of the mountains,
Between the sombre legions of cedars and tamaracks,
The rapids charge the ravine:
A little light, cast by foam under starlight,
Wavers about the shimmering stems of the birches:
Here rise up the clangorous sounds of battle,
Immense and mournful.
Far above curves the great dome of darkness
Drawn with the limitless lines of the stars and the planets.
Deep at the core of the tumult,
Deeper than all the voices that cry at the surface,
Dwells one fathomless sound,
Under the hiss and cry, the stroke and the plangent clamour.

O human heart that sleeps,
Wild with rushing dreams and deep with sadness!

The abysmal roar drops into almost silence,
While over its sleep play in various cadence
Innumerous voices crashing in laughter;
Then rising calm, overwhelming,
Slow in power,
Rising supreme in utterance,
It sways, and reconquers and floods all the spaces of silence,
One voice, deep with the sadness,
That dwells at the core of all things.
There by a nest in the glimmering birches,
Speaks a thrush as if startled from slumber,
Dreaming of Southern ricefields,
The moted glow of the amber sunlight,
Where the long ripple roves among the reeds.

Above curves the great dome of darkness,
Scored with the limitless lines of the stars and the planets;
Like the strong palm of God,
Veined with the ancient laws,
Holding a human heart that sleeps,
Wild with rushing dreams and deep with the sadness,
That dwells at the core of all things.

Night Hymns on Lake Nipigon

Here in the midnight, where the dark mainland and island
Shadows mingle in shadow deeper, profounder,
Sing we the hymns of the churches, while the dead water
        Whispers before us.

Thunder is travelling slow on the path of the lightning;
One after one the stars and the beaming planets
Look serene in the lake from the edge of the storm-cloud,
        Then have they vanished.

While our canoe, that floats dumb in the bursting thunder,
Gathers her voice in the quiet and thrills and whispers,
Presses her prow in the star-gleam, and all her ripple
        Lapses in blackness.

Sing we the sacred ancient hymns of the churches,
Chanted first in old-world nooks of the desert,
While in the wild, pellucid Nipigon reaches
        Hunted the savage.

Now have the ages met in the Northern midnight,
And on the lonely, loon-haunted Nipigon reaches
Rises the hymn of triumph and courage and comfort,
        Adeste Fideles.

Tones that were fashioned when the faith brooded in darkness,
Joined with sonorous vowels in the noble Latin,
Now are married with the long-drawn Ojibwa,
Uncouth and mournful.

Soft with the silver drip of the regular paddles
Falling in rhythm, timed with the liquid, plangent
Sounds from the blades where the whirlpools break and are carried
Down into darkness;

Each long cadence, flying like a dove from her shelter
Deep in the shadow, wheels for a throbbing moment,
Poises in utterance, returning in circles of silver
To nest in the silence.

All wild nature stirs with the infinite, tender
Plaint of a bygone age whose soul is eternal,
Bound in the lonely phrases that thrill and falter
Back into quiet.

Back they falter as the deep storm overtakes them,
Whelms them in splendid hollows of booming thunder,
Wraps them in rain, that, sweeping, breaks and onrushes
Ringing like cymbals.

On the Way to the Mission

They dogged him all one afternoon,
Through the bright snow,
Two whitemen servants of greed;
He knew that they were there,
But he turned not his head;
He was an Indian trapper;
He planted his snow-shoes firmly,
He dragged the long toboggan
Without rest.

The three figures drifted
Like shadows in the mind of a seer;
The snow-shoes were whisperers
On the threshold of awe;
The toboggan made the sound of wings,
A wood-pigeon sloping to her nest.

The Indian's face was calm.
He strode with the sorrow of fore-knowledge,
But his eyes were jewels of content
Set in circles of peace.

They would have shot him;
But momently in the deep forest,
They saw something flit by his side:
Their hearts stopped with fear.
Then the moon rose.
They would have left him to the spirit,
But they saw the long toboggan
Rounded well with furs,
With many a silver fox-skin,
With the pelts of mink and of otter.
They were the servants of greed;
When the moon grew brighter
And the spruces were dark with sleep,
They shot him.
When he fell on a shield of moonlight
One of his arms clung to his burden;
The snow was not melted:
The spirit passed away.

Then the servants of greed
Tore off the cover to count their gains;
They shuddered away into the shadows,
Hearing each the loud heart of the other.
Silence was born.

There in the tender moonlight,
    As sweet as they were in life,
Glimmered the ivory features,
    Of the Indian's wife.

In the manner of Montagnais women
    Her hair was rolled with braid;
Under her waxen fingers
    A crucifix was laid.

He was drawing her down to the Mission,
    To bury her there in spring,
When the bloodroot comes and the windflower
    To silver everything.

But as a gift of plunder
    Side by side were they laid,
The moon went on to her setting
    And covered them with shade.

The Wood Peewee

He comes in Springtime with the breeze
    That shakes the flowering maples,
He builds his nest in greening trees
    Where shower and sunshine dapples;
When all the woods are tranced and still,
    Amid the virgin leaves
His pensive note he sounds at will,
    He grieves.

At dawning when the cool air floats,
When dove-wing tints are streaming,
He, earliest of the early throats,
Begins his song adreaming;
While round his nest still clings the night,
He pipes in wistful flushes,
But when the wind lets in the light,
He hushes.

Yet is his heart with joyance filled
And not with brooding sadness;
If he might utter as he willed
His strain would mount in gladness;
It meaneth joy in simple trust,
Though pensively it rings;
Not as he would but as he must
He sings.

The Height of Land

Here is the height of land:
The watershed on either hand
Goes down to Hudson Bay
Or Lake Superior;
The stars are up, and far away
The wind sounds in the wood, wearier
Than the long Ojibwa cadence
In which Potàn the Wise
Declares the ills of life
And Chees-que-ne-ne makes a mournful sound
Of acquiescence. The fires burn low
With just sufficient glow
To light the flakes of ash that play
At being moths, and flutter away

To fall in the dark and die as ashes:
Here there is peace in the lofty air,
And Something comes by flashes
Deeper than peace;—
The spruces have retired a little space
And left a field of sky in violet shadow
With stars like marigolds in a water-meadow.

Now the Indian guides are dead asleep;
There is no sound unless the soul can hear
The gathering of the waters in their sources.

We have come up through the spreading lakes
From level to level,—
Pitching our tents sometimes over a revel
Of roses that nodded all night,
Dreaming within our dreams,
To wake at dawn and find that they were captured
With no dew on their leaves;
Sometimes mid sheaves
Of bracken and dwarf-cornel, and again
On a wide blueberry plain
Brushed with the shimmer of a bluebird's wing;
A rocky islet followed
With one lone poplar and a single nest
Of white-throat-sparrows that took no rest
But sang in dreams or woke to sing,—
To the last portage and the height of land—:
Upon one hand
The lonely north enlaced with lakes and streams,
And the enormous targe of Hudson Bay,
Glimmering all night
In the cold arctic light;
On the other hand
The crowded southern land

With all the welter of the lives of men.
But here is peace, and again
That Something comes by flashes
Deeper than peace,—a spell
Golden and inappellable
That gives the inarticulate part
Of our strange being one moment of release
That seems more native than the touch of time,
And we must answer in chime;
Though yet no man may tell
The secret of that spell
Golden and inappellable.

Now are there sounds walking in the wood,
And all the spruces shiver and tremble,
And the stars move a little in their courses.
The ancient disturber of solitude
Breathes a pervasive sigh,
And the soul seems to hear
The gathering of the waters at their sources;
Then quiet ensues and pure starlight and dark;
The region-spirit murmurs in meditation,
The heart replies in exaltation
And echoes faintly like an inland shell
Ghost tremors of the spell;
Thought reawakens and is linked again
With all the welter of the lives of men.
Here on the uplands where the air is clear
We think of life as of a stormy scene,—
Of tempest, of revolt and desperate shock;
And here, where we can think, on the bright uplands
Where the air is clear, we deeply brood on life
Until the tempest parts, and it appears
As simple as to the shepherd seems his flock:
A Something to be guided by ideals—

That in themselves are simple and serene—
Of noble deed to foster noble thought,
And noble thought to image noble deed,
Till deed and thought shall interpenetrate,
Making life lovelier, till we come to doubt
Whether the perfect beauty that escapes
Is beauty of deed or thought or some high thing
Mingled of both, a greater boon than either:
Thus we have seen in the retreating tempest
The victor-sunlight merge with the ruined rain,
And from the rain and sunlight spring the rainbow.

The ancient disturber of solitude
Stirs his ancestral potion in the gloom,
And the dark wood
Is stifled with the pungent fume
Of charred earth burnt to the bone
That takes the place of air.
Then sudden I remember when and where,—
The last weird lakelet foul with weedy growths
And slimy viscid things the spirit loathes,
Skin of vile water over viler mud
Where the paddle stirred unutterable stenches,
And the canoes seemed heavy with fear,
Not to be urged toward the fatal shore
Where a bush fire, smouldering, with sudden roar
Leaped on a cedar and smothered it with light
And terror. It had left the portage-height
A tangle of slanted spruces burned to the roots,
Covered still with patches of bright fire
Smoking with incense of the fragrant resin
That even then began to thin and lessen
Into the gloom and glimmer of ruin.

'Tis overpast. How strange the stars have grown;
The presage of extinction glows on their crests
And they are beautied with impermanence;
They shall be after the race of men
And mourn for them who snared their fiery pinions,
Entangled in the meshes of bright words.

A lemming stirs the fern and in the mosses
Eft-minded things feel the air change, and dawn
Tolls out from the dark belfries of the spruces.
How often in the autumn of the world
Shall the crystal shrine of dawning be rebuilt
With deeper meaning! Shall the poet then,
Wrapped in his mantle on the height of land,
Brood on the welter of the lives of men
And dream of his ideal hope and promise
In the blush sunrise? Shall he base his flight
Upon a more compelling law than Love
As Life's atonement; shall the vision
Of noble deed and noble thought immingled
Seem as uncouth to him as the pictograph
Scratched on the cave side by the cave-dweller
To us of the Christ-time? Shall he stand
With deeper joy, with more complex emotion,
In closer commune with divinity,
With the deep fathomed, with the firmament charted,
With life as simple as a sheep-boy's song,
What lies beyond a romaunt that was read
Once on a morn of storm and laid aside
Memorious with strange immortal memories?
Or shall he see the sunrise as I see it
In shoals of misty fire the deluge-light
Dashes upon and whelms with purer radiance,
And feel the lulled earth, older in pulse and motion,
Turn the rich lands and the inundant oceans

To the flushed color, and hear as now I hear
The thrill of life beat up the planet's margin
And break in the clear susurrus of deep joy
That echoes and reëchoes in my being?
O Life is intuition the measure of knowledge
And do I stand with heart entranced and burning
At the zenith of our wisdom when I feel
The long light flow, the long wind pause, the deep
Influx of spirit, of which no man may tell
The Secret, golden and inappellable?

Meditation at Perugia

The sunset colours mingle in the sky,
    And over all the Umbrian valleys flow;
    Trevi is touched with wonder, and the glow
Finds high Perugia crimson with renown;
        Spello is bright;
And, ah! St. Francis, thy deep-treasured town,
        Enshrined Assisi, fully fronts the light.

This valley knew thee many a year ago;
    Thy shrine was built by simpleness of heart;
    And from the wound called life thou drew'st the smart:
Unquiet kings came to thee and the sad poor—
        Thou gavest them peace;
Far as the Sultan and the Iberian shore
        Thy faith and abnegation gave release.

Deeper our faith, but not so sweet as thine;
    Wider our view, but not so sanely sure;
    For we are troubled by the witching lure
Of Science, with her lightning on the mist;
        Science that clears,
Yet never quite discloses what she wist,
        And leaves us half with doubts and half with fears.

We act her dreams that shadow forth the truth,
  That somehow here the very nerves of God
  Thrill the old fires, the rocks, the primal sod;
We throw our speech upon the open air,
    And it is caught
Far down the world, to sing and murmur there;
    Our common words are with deep wonder fraught.

Shall not the subtle spirit of man contrive
  To charm the tremulous ether of the soul,
  Wherein it breathes?—until, from pole to pole,
Those who are kin shall speak, as face to face,
    From star to star,
Even from earth to the most secret place,
    Where God and the supreme archangels are.

Shall we not prove, what thou hast faintly taught,
  That all the powers of earth and air are one,
  That one deep law persists from mole to sun?
Shall we not search the heart of God and find
    That law empearled,
Until all things that are in matter and mind
    Throb with the secret that began the world?

Yea, we have journeyed since thou trod'st the road,
  Yet still we keep the foreappointed quest;
  While the last sunset smoulders in the West,
Still the great faith with the undying hope
    Upsprings and flows,
While dim Assisi fades on the wide slope
    And the deep Umbrian valleys fill with rose.

Powassan's Drum

Throb—throb—throb—throb;—
Is this throbbing a sound
Or an ache in the air?
Pervasive as light,
Measured and inevitable,
It seems to float from no distance,
But to live in the listening world—
Throb—throb—throb—throb—throbbing
The sound of Powassan's Drum.

He crouches in his dwarf wigwam
Wizened with fasting,
Fierce with thirst,
Making great medicine
In memory of hated things dead
Or in menace of hated things to come,
And the universe listens
To the throb—throb—throb—throb—
Throbbing of Powassan's Drum.

The world seems lost and shallow,
Seems sunken and filled with water,
With shores lightly moving
Of marish grass and slender reeds.
Through it all goes
The throbbing of Powassan's Drum.

Has it gone on forever,
As the pulse of Being?
Will it last till the world's end
As the pulse of Being?
He crouches under the poles
Covered with strips of birchbark

And branches of poplar and pine,
Piled for shade and dying
In dense perfume,
With closed eyelids
With eyes so fierce,
Burning under and through
The ancient worn eyelids,
He crouches and beats his drum.

The morning star formed
Like a pearl in the shell of darkness;
Light welled like water from the springs of morning;
The stars in the earth shadow
Caught like whitefish in a net;
The sun, the fisherman,
Pulling the net to the shore of night,
Flashing with the fins of the caught stars;—
All to the throbbing of Powassan's Drum.

The live things in the world
Hear it and are silent.
They hide silent and charmed
As if guarding a secret;
Charmed and silent hiding a rich secret,
Throbbing all to the
Throb—throb—throbbing of Powassan's Drum.

Stealthy as death the water
Wanders in the long grass,
And spangs of sunlight
Slide on the slender reeds
Like beads of bright oil.
The sky is a bubble blown so tense
The blue has gone gray
Stretched to the throb—throb—throb—throb—
Throbbing of Powassan's Drum.

Is it a memory of hated things dead
That he beats—famished—
Or a menace of hated things to come
That he beats—parched with anger
And famished with hatred—?

The sun waited all day.
There was no answer.
He hauled his net
And the glint of the star-fins
Flashed in the water of twilight;
There was no answer.
But in the northeast
A storm cloud reaches like a hand
Out of the half darkness.
The spectral fingers of cloud
Grope in the heavens,
And at moments, sharp as pain,
A bracelet of bright fire
Plays on the wrist of the cloud.
Thunder from the hollow of the hand
Comes almost soundless, like an air pressure,
And the cloud rears up
To the throbbing of Powassan's Drum.
An infusion of bitter darkness
Stains the sweet water of twilight.

Then from the reeds stealing,
A shadow noiseless,
A canoe moves noiseless as sleep,
Noiseless as the trance of deep sleep
And an Indian still as a statue,
Molded out of deep sleep,
Headless, still as a headless statue
Molded out of deep sleep,
Sits modelled in full power,

Haughty in manful power,
Headless and impotent in power.
The canoe stealthy as death
Drifts to the throbbing of Powassan's Drum.
The Indian fixed like bronze
Trails his severed head
Through the dead water
Holding it by the hair,
By the plaits of hair,
Wound with sweet grass and tags of silver.
The face looks through the water
Up to its throne on the shoulders of power,
Unquenched eyes burning in the water,
Piercing beyond the shoulders of power
Up to the fingers of the storm cloud.

Is this the meaning of the magic—
The translation into sight
Of the viewless hate?
Is this what the world waited for
As it listened to the throb—throb—throb—throb—
Throbbing of Powassan's Drum?

The sun could not answer.
The tense sky burst and went dark
And could not answer.
But the storm answers.
The murdered shadow sinks in the water.
Uprises the storm
And crushes the dark world;
At the core of the rushing fury
Bursting hail, tangled lightning
Wind in a wild vortex
Lives the triumphant throb—throb—throb—throb—
Throbbing of Powassan's Drum.

September

The morns are grey with haze and faintly cold,
The early sunsets arc the west with red;
The stars are misty silver overhead,
Above the dawn Orion lies outrolled.
Now all the slopes are slowly growing gold,
And in the dales a deeper silence dwells;
The crickets mourn with funeral flutes and bells,
For days before the summer had grown old.

Now the night-gloom with hurrying wings is stirred,
Strangely the comrade pipings rise and sink,
The birds are following in the pathless dark
The footsteps of the pilgrim summer. Hark!
Was that the redstart or the bobolink?
That lonely cry the summer-hearted bird?

In the Country Churchyard

To the Memory of My Father

This is the acre of unfathomed rest,
These stones, with weed and lichen bound, enclose
No active grief, no uncompleted woes,
But only finished work and harboured quest,
And balm for ills;
And the last gold that smote the ashen west
Lies garnered here between the harvest hills.

This spot has never known the heat of toil,
Save when the angel with the mighty spade
Has turned the sod and built the house of shade;
But here old chance is guardian of the soil;

Green leaf and grey,
The barrows blossom with the tangled spoil,
And God's own weeds are fair in God's own way.

Sweet flowers may gather in the ferny wood:
Hepaticas, the morning stars of spring;
The bloodroots with their milder ministering,
Like planets in the lonelier solitude;
And that white throng,
Which shakes the dingles with a starry brood,
And tells the robin his forgotten song.

These flowers may rise amid the dewy fern,
They may not root within this antique wall,
The dead have chosen for their coronal,
No buds that flaunt of life and flare and burn;
They have agreed,
To choose a beauty puritan and stern,
The universal grass, the homely weed.

This is the paradise of common things,
The scourged and trampled here find peace to grow,
The frost to furrow and the wind to sow,
The mighty sun to time their blossomings;
And now they keep
A crown reflowering on the tombs of kings,
Who earned their triumph and have claimed their sleep.

Yea, each is here a prince in his own right,
Who dwelt disguised amid the multitude,
And when his time was come, in haughty mood,
Shook off his motley and reclaimed his might;
His sombre throne
In the vast province of perpetual night,
He holds secure, inviolate, alone.

The poor forgets that ever he was poor,
  The priest has lost his science of the truth,
  The maid her beauty, and the youth his youth,
The statesman has forgot his subtle lure,
    The old his age,
The sick his suffering, and the leech his cure,
    The poet his perplexed and vacant page.

These swains that tilled the uplands in the sun
  Have all forgot the field's familiar face,
  And lie content within this ancient place,
Whereto when hands were tired their thought would run
    To dream of rest,
When the last furrow was turned down, and won
    The last harsh harvest from the earth's patient breast.

O dwellers in the valley vast and fair,
  I would that calling from your tranquil clime,
  You make a truce for me with cruel time;
For I am weary of this eager care
    That never dies;
I would be born into your tranquil air,
    Your deserts crowned and sovereign silences.

I would, but that the world is beautiful,
  And I am more in love with the sliding years,
  They have not brought me frantic joy or tears,
But only moderate state and temperate rule;
    Not to forget
This quiet beauty, not to be Time's fool,
    I will be man a little longer yet.

For lo, what beauty crowns the harvest hills!—
  The buckwheat acres gleam like silver shields;
  The oats hang tarnished in the golden fields;

Between the elms the yellow wheat-land fills;
The apples drop
Within the orchard, where the red tree spills,
The fragrant fruitage over branch and prop.

The cows go lowing through the lovely vale;
The clarion peacock warns the world of rain,
Perched on the barn a gaudy weather-vane;
The farm lad holloes from the shifted rail,
Along the grove
He beats a measure on his ringing pail,
And sings the heart-song of his early love.

There is a honey scent along the air;
The hermit thrush has tuned his fleeting note,
Among the silver birches far remote
His spirit voice appeareth here and there,
To fail and fade,
A visionary cadence falling fair,
That lifts and lingers in the hollow shade.

And now a spirit in the east, unseen,
Raises the moon above her misty eyes,
And travels up the veiled and starless skies,
Viewing the quietude of her demesne;
Stainless and slow,
I watch the lustre of her planet's sheen,
From burnished gold to liquid silver flow,

And now I leave the dead with you, O night;
You wear the semblance of their fathomless state,
For you we long when the day's fire is great,
And when stern life is cruellest in his might,
Of death we dream:
A country of dim plain and shadowy height,
Crowned with strange stars and silences supreme:

Rest here, for day is hot to follow you,
   Rest here until the morning star has come,
   Until is risen aloft dawn's rosy dome,
Based deep on buried crimson into blue,
      And morn's desire
Has made the fragile cobweb drenched with dew
      A net of opals veiled with dreamy fire.

The First Snow

I

The field pools gathered into frosted lace;
   An icy glitter lined the iron ruts,
   And bound the circle of the musk-rat huts;
A junco flashed about a sunny space
Where rose stems made a golden amber grace;
   Between the dusky alders' woven ranks,
   A stream thought yet about his summer banks,
And made an August music in the place.

Along the horizon's faded shrunken lines,
   Veiling the gloomy borders of the night,
      Hung the great snow clouds washed with pallid gold;
And stealing from his covert in the pines,
   The wind, encouraged to a stinging flight,
      Dropped in the hollow conquered by the cold.

II

Then a light cloud rose up for hardihood,
   Trailing a veil of snow that whirled and broke,
   Blown softly like a shroud of steam or smoke,
Sallied across a knoll where maples stood,

Charged over broken country for a rood,
   Then seeing the night withdrew his force and fled,
   Leaving the ground with snow-flakes thinly spread,
And traces of the skirmish in the wood.

The stars sprang out and flashed serenely near,
   The solid frost came down with might and main,
   It set the rivers under bolt and bar;
Bang! went the starting eaves beneath the strain,
   And e'er Orion saw the morning-star
The winter was the master of the year.

Watkwenies

Vengeance was once her nation's lore and law:
When the tired sentry stooped above the rill,
Her long knife flashed, and hissed, and drank its fill;
Dimly below her dripping wrist she saw,
One wild hand, pale as death and weak as straw,
Clutch at the ripple in the pool; while shrill
Sprang through the dreaming hamlet on the hill,
The war-cry of the triumphant Iroquois.

Now clothed with many an ancient flap and fold,
And wrinkled like an apple kept till May,
She weighs the interest-money in her palm,
And, when the Agent calls her valiant name,
Hears, like the war-whoops of her perished day,
The lads playing snow-snake in the stinging cold.

Off Riviere Du Loup

O ship incoming from the sea
  With all your cloudy tower of sail,
Dashing the water to the lee,
  And leaning grandly to the gale;

The sunset pageant in the west
  Has filled your canvas curves with rose,
And jewelled every toppling crest
  That crashes into silver snows!

You know the joy of coming home,
  After long leagues to France or Spain;
You feel the clear Canadian foam
  And the gulf water heave again.

Between these sombre purple hills
  That cool the sunset's molten bars,
You will go on as the wind wills,
  Beneath the river's roof of stars.

You will toss onward toward the lights
  That spangle over the lonely pier,
By hamlets glimmering on the heights,
  By level islands black and clear.

You will go on beyond the tide,
  Through brimming plains of olive sedge,
Through paler shallows light and wide,
  The rapids piled along the ledge.

At evening off some reedy bay
  You will swing slowly on your chain,
And catch the scent of dewy hay,
  Soft blowing from the pleasant plain.

At Les Eboulements

The bay is set with ashy sails,
With purple shades that fade and flee,
And curling by in silver wales,
The tide is straining from the sea.

The grassy points are slowly drowned,
The water laps and over-rolls,
The wicker pêche; with shallow sound
A light wave labours on the shoals.

The crows are feeding in the foam,
They rise in crowds tumultuously,
'Come home,' they cry, 'come home, come home,
And leave the marshes to the sea.'

Night and the Pines

Here in the pine shade is the nest of night,
Lined deep with shadows, odorous and dim,
And here he stays his sweeping flight,
Here where the strongest wind is lulled for him,
He lingers brooding until dawn,
While all the trembling stars move on and on.

Under the cliff there drops a lonely fall,
Deep and half heard its thunder lifts and booms;
Afar the loons with eerie call
Haunt all the bays, and breaking through the glooms
Upfloats that cry of light despair,
As if a demon laughed upon the air.

A raven croaks from out his ebon sleep,
　　When a brown cone falls near him through the dark;
And when the radiant meteors sweep
　　Afar within the larches wakes the lark;
　　　　The wind moves on the cedar hill,
　　　　Tossing the weird cry of the whip-poor-will.

Sometimes a titan wind, slumbrous and hushed,
　　Takes the dark grove within his swinging power;
And like a cradle softly pushed,
　　The shade sways slowly for a lulling hour;
　　　　While through the cavern sweeps a cry,
　　　　A Sibyl with her secret prophecy.

When morning lifts its fragile silver dome,
　　And the first eagle takes the lonely air,
Up from his dense and sombre home
　　The night sweeps out, a tireless wayfarer,
　　　　Leaving within the shadows deep,
　　　　The haunting mood and magic of his sleep.

And so we cannot come within this grove,
　　But all the quiet dusk remembrance brings
Of ancient sorrow and of hapless love,
　　Fate, and the dream of power, and piercing things
　　　　Traces of mystery and might,
　　　　The passion-sadness of the soul of night.

Sophia M. Almon Hensley

Sophia Margaretta Almon Hensley was born on May 31, 1866 in Bridgetown, Nova Scotia. Although Canadian born, she was educated largely in England (St. Monica's School in Warwickshire) and Paris. Indeed, she lived for the most part in New York, England, and on the Channel Islands. Hensley did, however, often visit her native Nova Scotia during the summers, St. Marys Bay being one of her favourite spots. After a long life she retired to Windsor, Nova Scotia, where she died on February 10, 1946.

While Hensley was the last born of our sixteen poets, she was a protégé of Sir Charles G.D. Roberts, and he opened a few doors for her. Her first collection, *Poems*, was published as early as 1889. Like all poets living on or near the Bay of Fundy, she wrote about the marshlands in poems like "Slack Tide" from her aforementioned *Poems*. In addition to her nature poetry, like several other Confederation Poets, Hensley was deeply concerned about the erosion of Christian faith that was part of the *fin de siècle* ethos of the late nineteenth century.

Noon

No ripple stirs the water,
   No song-bird wakes the grove,
Calm noontide sways his sceptre
   And hushes even love.

On earth the sun-god bending
   Poureth his wondrous store,
The soft-tongued tide, advancing,
   Laps the unconscious shore.

The long low isle of marsh-land
   Stretches in weary waste,
By sloping sand-banks guarded,
   By winding weeds embraced.

Comes clearly from the open
   The plash of distant oars,
Over the rocky headland
   The snowy sea-gull soars.

I see as if through dream-clouds,
   I hear from far away,
The scorched air breathes its opiate,
   The drowsy fancies stay.

I have no hopes nor longings,
   I scarce can feel your kiss,—
For thought, and joy, and worship
   Another hour than this!

Consecrated

Wild thunder bursting from a gracious sky,
    Devouring flames in peaceful village ways;
These have I known as, sweet with mystery,
    I see Love's new-born days.

Love is no perfumed plaything of the weak!
    The sobs that shook you as a storm-swept tree,
The hush, and my wet bosom, served to speak
    A strong man's agony.

Oh, Heart of mine, gone is the wild world's din,
    Gone the self-love and soilure of the years.
I looked and saw myself enshrined within
    The crystal of your tears!

At Ebb

A lull in the fitful fever of the year.
    A day of stillness. O'er the sleeping pools
        The darting swallow flickers on the wing
    Catching her image. Where the cliff-side cools
            A thousand quiet rivulets find the sea.
            The towering mountain frowns immovably
        Waiting the darkness; for the wild birds sing
Her forest follies when the dawn is near.

The madcap sea has donned a robe of gray,
    Playing the nun. Wide-eyed and innocent
        She lies, a fitting patience in her mien.
    When in the day's deploy her mood is spent
            How she will fling the mumming garment by,
            And joy to give her wild tempestuous cry,
        And bathe her white arms in the sunlight's sheen,
And mock the shore beguiled by her mad play.

Far off a hoarse gull screams; from out the bush
Of tangled alders sail white-breasted birds
Winnowing seaward; and along the beach
Runs the sandpiper. Strange, unuttered words
Lurk in the cryptal quiet of the wind.
Where the fog's fumid curtain is unpinned
Earth waits the birth-throe. Far as eye can reach
There is no shudder in the noonday hush.

I am of thee, O patient, smiling earth!
I am thy sister, O thou changing sea!
I bring my full-grown sorrow to thine ears,
O brooding mother! and the mystery
Of worn-out passions to thine endless calm.
Against thy cool glad face my fevered palm,
On thy sweet sod my fruitless, satiate tears,
There, too, my mad remembrances of mirth.

The Turning of the Tide

Green and glad the mysteries
Of the woodland sheen and shade,
And the thousand gleaming eyes
Of the daisies in the glade.

Towards the hoar wave-beaten rock
Creeps the tireless, stealthy sea,
Stern her voice, and rude the shock,
Yet he will not quake nor flee.

West the blue horizon line
Fades into an opal dream,
And the smoke-wreaths curl and twine
Like a wandering mountain stream.

Fresh and sweet the sea-blown gale,
    Cool the fogs that close and cling,
White the chaff that flies the flail
    In great ocean's winnowing.

Mine the sight, but not the sense;
    I have grown a thing apart;
Gone the old sweet confidence,
    And the unison of heart.

And I stretch my eager hands
    Calling to the vast unknown:
"Give me back my dream-tide lands,
    And my dear, deserted throne!

Take the things the heart has craved,
    Gained, and hoarded for a space,
Sweets of fears my soul has braved,
    And the glory of a face;

Unnamed gladnesses of night,
    Joys of wine, and warmth, and love,
All my memories of delight,
    All my power to hold and move;

Give me back the unsung ways,
    My wild kinship with the wind;
And the dear, deep-hearted days
    I have left so far behind.

Let me hear the lonely rune
    Of the wind-birds in the west,
Hear the ocean-mother croon
    To the darlings at her breast;

Know that they and I have part
In all things that are, or seem,
In the universal Heart
And the interminable Dream."

Soft against the cooling sand
Presses close the scarlet cheek;
From the spirit's listless hand
Slip the gains that toilers seek;

Sounds of surf-beat in my ears,
On my hair the wind's impress;
And I know the bygone years,
And the old childheartedness.

The Meaning of the Bird Song

A desert of weary gray;
The endless wash on the shore;
Foam of an æon of fret and fray
Flung on the floor.

Shudder of laboring life,
Quiver of nesting birds;
Sombre the mantle of ceaseless strife
That daylight girds.

Ah, listen! Soft and low,
Joys, darting, lift and sink,
Soft wilding waters that fall and flow,
The bobolink!

Gladness of summer rain,
  Wild songs of shore and sod;
Over the swelling summer grain
  The hands of God.

Winds' will and ocean's roar,
  Red cliff and dewy haze,
The growl of the surf on the distant shore,
  Morn's blues and grays;

And the chime of impatient bells.
  See the breeze ruffle the lake!
And the drowsy day trembles through the dells,—
  The world is awake!

Pink palms and dimpled feet;
  Rosy mouth, dewy pressed,
Soft wandering, seeks the sweet
  Of Mother's breast.

Proud power of unsated strength,
  Staunch spars and sails unfurled,
Joy in the leagues of earth's unknown length,
  The will of a world.

Deep in the seedless sand,
  Through dirges of the pine,
In the fierce strength of the ploughman's hand
  A mote divine.

Slumbers the silent sod
  Waiting the spark, the ray,
Deep in the heart of the formless pod
  A dream of Day.

Clear flame of golden fire,
  Heaven's flash the soul has caught;
Far on the mount of the heart's desire
  The throne of Thought.

Glad life of lessons learned,
  Sweet love to teach and tend;
And the altars of stone where the self has burned.
  The strife is at end.

Love, and a great desire,—
  The urging of homeward waves;
And high on the mountain the dome of fire
  O'er the quiet caves.

The Soul

Enshrouded in a veil of morning mist
  The great cliff stands. About her base the waves
  Beat ceaselessly, and the wild north-wind raves
And the gray sea-gulls hover as they list.

There is no dream of fellowship, nor fear,
    In that great isolation. From the sea
    Wash through the mighty caves of mystery
The gems of silence. Crystalline and clear

Her summit's ether. Where the sweet rills run
Her steadfast bosom fronts the rising sun.

Returned

Back from the country—in the town once more!
No more the shy things of the woods I meet,
No more the fragrant pines my nostrils greet;
I only dream of standing on the shore,
The while the waves break round me with a roar.
The pavement echoes hard beneath my feet,
The houses shut me in both sides the street,
Companionship with sun-set hours is o'er.

But there are fairer things than summer moon
Rising or setting—than or hills or sky—
Sweeter than evening's glow or morning dew;
There's music dearer than the fairy tune
The winds play on the sea; and—blessed I!
I find them in the city here with you!

Northwest Wind

The blue sky, like an autumn threshing floor,
Was by the northwest wind swept clean and clear;
And westward through the lucent atmosphere
The far-off hills, the valley watching o'er
Became familiar neighbors at my door.
Within the soughing pine-tops I could hear
The hurrying footsteps of the winds pass near
In fleet race from the mountains to the shore.

And as the winds from out the clear northwest
Blew every vapor till the bracing air
Filled me with life, and built the world anew,
So by new vigor is my soul possessed,
And all my inner sky is clear and fair;
I find the rousing breath of life in you.

Somewhere in France

1918

Leave me alone here, proudly, with my dead,
  Ye mothers of brave sons adventurous;
He who once prayed: "If it be possible
  Let this cup pass" will arbitrate for us.
Your boy with iron nerves and careless smile
  Marched gaily by and dreamed of glory's goal;
Mine had blanched cheek, straight mouth and close-gripped hands
  And prayed that somehow he might save his soul.
I do not grudge your ribbon or your cross,
  The price of these my soldier, too, has paid;
I hug a prouder knowledge to my heart,
  The mother of the boy who was afraid!

He was a tender child with nerves so keen
  They doubled pain and magnified the sad;
He hated cruelty and things obscene
  And in all high and holy things was glad.
And so he gave what others could not give,
  The one supremest sacrifice he made,
A thing your brave boy could not understand;
  He gave his all because he was afraid!

Textual Notes

During the editing of this anthology, seventeen errors were discovered in the original copy-texts. These mistakes occurred in spelling and/or punctuation. All were silently corrected in the foregoing test. Here is a record of the changes that were made.

Isabella Valancy Crawford

Muskellunge is misspelled in Line 41 of "The Dark Stag" (the copy-text has muskallunge).

Grim is misspelled in Line 51 of "War" (the copy-text has Grin).

Barry Straton

Mermen's has the apostrophe in the wrong place in Line 14 of "Sunset on the Ocean" (the copy-text has mermens').

William Douw Lighthall

Passchendaele is misspelled in Lines 7, 22, and 29 of "Deathless" (the copy-text has Passchendale).

Also in "Deathless," readers will note two dates. At the beginning of the poem there is October 30, 1917. At the end of the poem there is February 3, 1918. Both dates are in the copy-text.

S. Frances Harrison

The editor and the publisher realize that Harrison's French in her poem "At St. Hilaire" is incorrect. Her poem, as presented in this anthology, is exactly as it appears in the copy-text.

Wilfred Campbell

There should be a comma after "sweet" in Line 15 of "Alone" (the copy-text has a period).

"Its" is misspelled in Line 3 of "Infancy" (the copy-text has "it's").

Charles G.D. Roberts

Dyke was spelled "dike" in Line 44 of "Tantramar Revisited" and has been changed to make it consistent with the rest of the poem.

Helena Coleman

The copy-text of her poem "And They Were Young" has no apostrophe at the start of Line 1. This has been added.

Nation's has the apostrophe in the wrong place in Line 32 of "Autumn, 1917" (the copy-text has nations').

E. Pauline Johnson (Tekahionwake)

The copy-text of her poem "Brier" has no period at the end of the poem. This has been added.

The copy-text of her poem "And He Said, Fight On" has a period at the end of Line 1 where it should have a comma. This has been corrected.

Archibald Lampman

Weird is misspelled in Line 25 of "In October" (the copy-text has wierd).

Duncan Campbell Scott

Where is misspelled in Line 27 of "Night Hymns on Lake Nipigon" (the copy-text has were).

The copy-text failed to indent Line 28 of "Meditation at Perugia" properly. This has been corrected.

The editor and the publisher realize that the title of Scott's poem, "Off Riviere Du Loup," contains incorrect French. The title should read: "Off Rivière-du-Loup." His poem, as presented in this anthology, is exactly as it appears in the copy-text.

Sophia M. Almon Hensley

In "The Turning of the Tide," the long passage in quotation marks that starts on Line 23 ("Give me back ...) should terminate at the end of Line 44, but the close quotation mark is missing in the copy-text. This has been added.

While the texts of the poems are as the poets wanted them to be, including unusual punctuation and capitalization, titles and subtitles have been standardized.

Copy-Texts

George Frederick Cameron

All poems are from *Lyrics on Freedom, Love and Death.* Cameron, Charles J., ed. Kingston, Ontario: Lewis W. Shannon, 1887 and Boston: Alexander Moore, 1887. Print.

Wilfred Campbell

"To the Lakes," "The Tides of Dawn," "Medwayosh," "On Christmas Eve," "Alone," and "Infancy" are from *Lake Lyrics and Other Poems.* Saint John, New Brunswick: J. & A. McMillan, 1889. Print.

All other Campbell poems are from *The Poems of Wilfred Campbell.* Toronto: William Briggs, 1905. Print.

Bliss Carman

"A Windflower," "A Sea-Drift," "A Northern Vigil," "The Eavesdropper," and "The Vagabonds" are from *Low Tide on Grand Pré: A Book of Lyrics.* Cambridge & Chicago: Stone and Kimball, 1894. Print. [Initially published by Charles L. Webster of New York in 1893.]

"Legends of Lost Haven" and "The Shadow Boatswain" are from *Ballads of Lost Haven: A Book of the Sea.* Boston: Lamson, Wolffe, 1897. Print.

All other Carman poems are from *Later Poems.* Toronto: McClelland & Stewart, 1921. Print.

Helena Coleman

"Give Me No Pity," "I am Content with Canada," "Love's Seasons," "The Guardians of the Place," "The Voices of Our Day," "When Autumn Comes," "Night Among the Thousand Islands," "In

October," "At Sunset," "Night," and "The Evening Hour" are from *Songs and Sonnets*. Toronto: The Tennyson Club of Toronto/ William Briggs, 1906. Print.

"The Day He Went," "And They Were Young," "Autumn, 1917," and "Convocation Hall" are from *Marching Men: War Verses*. Toronto: J.M. Dent, 1917. Print.

Isabella Valancy Crawford

All poems are from *The Collected Poems of Isabella Valancy Crawford*. Garvin, J.W., ed. Toronto: William Briggs, 1905. Print.

S. Frances Harrison

"Nocturne," "At St. Hilaire," "Tintern Abbey," "November," and "The Tree" are from *Pine, Rose and Fleur de Lis*. Toronto: Hart & Company, 1890. Print.

"In March," "The Marshes," and "At Valois" are from *In Northern Skies, and Other Poems*. Toronto: privately published, 1912. Print.

Sophia M. Almon Hensley

All poems except one are from *The Heart of a Woman*. New York: G.P. Putnam's Sons, 1906. Print.

"Somewhere in France" is from: Gerson, Carole and Gwendolyn Davies, eds. *Canadian Poetry: From the Beginnings Through the First World War*. Toronto: McClelland & Stewart, 1994. Print.

John Frederic Herbin

All poems are from *The Marshlands and The Trail of the Tide*. Toronto: William Briggs, 1899. Print.

E. Pauline Johnson (Tekahionwake)

All poems are from *Flint and Feather*. Toronto: Musson Book Co., 1912. Print.

Archibald Lampman

"Heat," "Among the Timothy," "In October," and "Solitude" are from *Among the Millet, and Other Poems*. Ottawa: J. Durie and Son, 1888. Print.

"At the Ferry," "September," and "An Autumn Landscape" are from *Lyrics of Earth*. Boston: Copeland & Day, 1895. Print.

All other Lampman poems are from *The Poems of Archibald Lampman*. Scott, Duncan Campbell, ed. Fourth Edition. Toronto: Musson Book Co. Print. [Initially published by George N. Morang of Toronto in 1900.]

William Douw Lighthall

All poems are from *Old Measures: Collected Verse*. Montreal: A.T. Chapman, 1922 and Toronto: Musson Book Co., 1922. Print.

Charles G.D. Roberts

All poems except one are from *Poems: New Complete Edition*. Toronto: The Copp, Clark Co., 1907. Print.

"My Trees" is from *Songs of the Common Day and Ave!: An Ode for the Shelley Centenary*. London and New York: Longmans, Green, and Co., 1893. Print.

Duncan Campbell Scott

All poems are from *The Poems of Duncan Campbell Scott*. Toronto: McClelland & Stewart, 1926. Print.

Frederick George Scott

All poems are from *Collected Poems*. Vancouver: Clarke & Stuart, 1934. Print.

Barry Straton

All poems except one are from *Lays of Love, and Miscellaneous Poems*. Saint John, New Brunswick: J. & A. McMillan, 1884. Print.

"A Dream Fulfilled" is from: Lighthall, William Douw, ed. *Songs of the Great Dominion: Voices from the Forests and Waters, the*

Settlements and Cities of Canada. London: Walter Scott, "Windsor Series," 1889. Print.

Ethelwyn Wetherald

All poems are from *The Last Robin: Lyrics and Sonnets*. Toronto: William Briggs, 1907. Print.

Bibliography

Books by the sixteen Confederation Poets:

George Frederick Cameron

Lyrics on Freedom, Love and Death. Cameron, Charles J., ed. Kingston, Ontario: Lewis W. Shannon, 1887 and Boston: Alexander Moore, 1887. Print. (Facsimile edition by Facsimile Publisher, India.)

Wilfred Campbell

Beyond the Hills of Dream. Boston: The Riverside Press/Houghton Mifflin, 1899. Print. (Facsimile edition by Pranava Books, India.)

The Dread Voyage. Toronto: William Briggs, 1893. Print.

Lake Lyrics and Other Poems. Saint John, New Brunswick: J. & A. McMillan, 1889. Print. (Facsimile edition by Pranava Books, India.)

The Poems of Wilfred Campbell. Published in a limited edition as *The Collected Poems of Wilfred Campbell* for the members of The Canadian Club of Toronto by William Briggs, 1905. Print.

Snowflakes and Sunbeams. St. Stephen, New Brunswick: *The Saint Croix Courier* Press, 1888. Print. (Facsimile edition by Facsimile Publisher, India.)

Vapour and Blue: Souster selects Campbell: the poetry of William Wilfred Campbell. Souster, Raymond, ed. Sutton West, Ontario: The Paget Press, 1978. Print.

Bliss Carman

Ballads of Lost Haven: A Book of the Sea. Boston: Lamson, Wolffe, 1897. Print. (Facsimile edition by Skilled Books, India.)

Later Poems. Toronto: McClelland & Stewart, 1921. Print.

Low Tide on Grand Pré: A Book of Lyrics. Cambridge & Chicago: Stone and Kimball, 1894. Print. [Initially published by Charles L. Webster of New York in 1893.] (Facsimile edition by Pranava Books, India.)

Windflower: Poems of Bliss Carman. Souster, Raymond and Douglas Lochhead, eds. Ottawa: Tecumseh Press, 1985. Print.

Helena Coleman

Marching Men: War Verses. Toronto: J.M. Dent, 1917. Print. (Facsimile edition by Skilled Books, India.)

Songs and Sonnets. Toronto: The Tennyson Club of Toronto/William Briggs, 1906. Print. (Facsimile edition by Pranava Books, India.)

Isabella Valancy Crawford

The Collected Poems of Isabella Valancy Crawford. Garvin, J.W., ed. Toronto: William Briggs, 1905. Print. (Facsimile edition, with a new "Introduction" by James Reaney, published as *Collected Poems*. Toronto: University of Toronto Press, 1972. Print.)

S. Frances Harrison

In Northern Skies, and Other Poems. Toronto: privately published, 1912. Print. (Facsimile edition by Pranava Books, India.)

Pine, Rose and Fleur de Lis. Toronto: Hart & Company, 1890. Print. (Facsimile edition by Pranava Books, India.)

Sophia M. Almon Hensley

The Heart of a Woman. New York: G.P. Putnam's Sons, 1906. Print. (Facsimile edition by Pranava Books, India.)

Poems. Windsor, Nova Scotia: J.J. Anslow, 1889. Print. (Reprint edition from: Book Depository International, England.)

A Woman's Love Letters. New York: J. Selwyn Tait and Sons, 1895. Print. (Facsimile edition by Pranava Books, India.)

John Frederic Herbin

The Marshlands and The Trail of the Tide. Toronto: William Briggs, 1899. Print. (Facsimile edition by Franklin Classics, U.S.A.)

E. Pauline Johnson (Tekahionwake)

Canadian Born. Toronto: George N. Morang, 1903. Print.

Flint and Feather. Toronto: Musson Book Co., 1912. Print. (Reprint edition, with a new "Biographical Sketch," by PaperJacks/General Publishing in 1972.)

The White Wampum. London: The Bodley Head, 1895. Print.

Archibald Lampman

Alcyone, and Other Poems. Ottawa: James Ogilvy, 1899. Print.

Among the Millet, and Other Poems. Ottawa: J. Durie and Son, 1888. Print. (Facsimile edition by Pranava Books, India.)

At the Long Sault, And Other New Poems. Collected by Duncan Campbell Scott and E.K. Brown. Toronto: The Ryerson Press, 1943. Print.

Comfort of the Fields: Archibald Lampman, The best-known Poems. Souster, Raymond, ed. Sutton West, Ontario: The Paget Press, 1979. Print.

Lyrics of Earth. Boston: Copeland & Day, 1895. Print. (Facsimile edition by Facsimile Publisher, India.)

The Poems of Archibald Lampman. Scott, Duncan Campbell, ed. Fourth Edition. Toronto: Musson Book Co. Print. [Initially published by George N. Morang of Toronto in 1900.] (Facsimile edition by Facsimile Publisher, India.)

William Douw Lighthall

Old Measures: Collected Verse. Montreal: A.T. Chapman, 1922 and Toronto: Musson Book Co., 1922. Print. (Facsimile edition by Pranava Books, India.)

Charles G.D. Roberts

The Book of the Native. Toronto: The Copp, Clark Co., 1896. Print. (Facsimile edition by Pranava Books, India.)

The Book of the Rose. Boston: L.C. Page, 1903. Print.

In Diverse Tones. Boston: D. Lathrop and Company, 1886. Print. (Reprint edition from: Book Depository International, England.)

New York Nocturnes And Other Poems. Boston: Lamson, Wolffe, 1898 and Boston: L.C. Page, 1898. Print.

Poems: New Complete Edition. Toronto: The Copp, Clark Co., 1907. Print.

The Selected Poems of Sir Charles G.D. Roberts. Pacey, Desmond, ed. Toronto: The Ryerson Press, 1955. Print.

Songs of the Common Day and Ave!: An Ode for the Shelley Centenary. London and New York: Longmans, Green, and Co., 1893. Print. (Facsimile edition by Bibliolife, U.S.A.)

Duncan Campbell Scott

Lundy's Lane, and Other Poems. New York: George H. Doran Company, 1916. Print. (Facsimile edition by Forgotten Books, England.)

New World Lyrics and Ballads. Toronto: George N. Morang, 1905. Print. (Facsimile edition by Pranava Books, India.)

The Poems of Duncan Campbell Scott. Toronto: McClelland & Stewart, 1926. Print.

Powassan's Drum: Poems of Duncan Campbell Scott. Souster, Raymond and Douglas Lochhead, eds. Ottawa: Tecumseh Press, 1985. Print.

Via Borealis. Toronto: Wm. Tyrrell & Co., 1906. Print. (Facsimile edition by Pranava Books, India.)

Frederick George Scott

Collected Poems. Vancouver: Clarke & Stuart, 1934. Print.

Barry Straton

Lays of Love, and Miscellaneous Poems. Saint John, New Brunswick: J. & A. McMillan, 1884. Print. (Facsimile edition by Pranava Books, India.)

Ethelwyn Wetherald

The Last Robin: Lyrics and Sonnets. Toronto: William Briggs, 1907. Print. (Facsimile edition by Pranava Books, India.)

Major Anthologies containing Works by the Confederation Poets:

Atwood, Margaret, ed. *The New Oxford Book of Canadian Verse in English.* Toronto: Oxford University Press, 1982. Print.

Burpee, Lawrence J., ed. *A Century of Canadian Sonnets.* Toronto: Musson Book Co., 1910. Print. (Facsimile edition by Facsimile Publisher, India.)

Campbell, Wilfred, ed. *The Oxford Book of Canadian Verse.* Toronto: Oxford University Press, 1913. Print. (Facsimile edition, with a new "Introduction" by Len Early, published by OUP in 2013. Print.)

David, Jack and Robert Lecker, eds. *Canadian Poetry, Volume One.* Toronto: General Publishing, 1982. Print.

Garvin, John W., ed. *Canadian Poets.* Toronto: McClelland, Goodchild & Stewart, 1916. Print.

Gerson, Carole and Gwendolyn Davies, eds. *Canadian Poetry: From the Beginnings Through the First World War.* Toronto: McClelland & Stewart, 1994. Print.

Gustafson, Ralph, ed. *The Penguin Book of Canadian Verse.* Harmondsworth, Middlesex, England: Penguin Books, 1967 (revised edition). Print.

Klinck, C.F. and R.E. Watters, eds. *Canadian Anthology.* Toronto: W.J. Gage, 1955. Print.

Lighthall, William Douw, ed. *Songs of the Great Dominion: Voices from the Forests and Waters, the Settlements and Cities of Canada.* London: Walter Scott, "Windsor Series," 1889. Print.

Lochhead, Douglas and Raymond Souster, eds. *100 Poems of Nineteenth Century Canada.* Toronto: Macmillan of Canada, 1974. Print.

Rand, Theodore H., ed. *A Treasury of Canadian Verse.* New York: E.P. Dutton and London: J.M. Dent, 1900. Print.

Ross, Malcolm, ed. *Poets of the Confederation.* Toronto: McClelland & Stewart, 1960. Print.

Acknowledgments

The creation of a representative selection of the finest poetry written by the most important of our Confederation Poets requires the support of a collaborative team. I am thankful for the work of Shona Deahl, Terry Barker, Katherine L. Gordon, Norma West Linder, and my friends and colleagues at Guernica Editions.

I am deeply indebted to Shona Deahl for her editorial consulting during the selection process. Her sharp eyes, displayed during her stylistic and copyediting of my manuscript, and her timely suggestions were valuable. Shona also conducted crucial internet research. She is the best proofreader I know.

Special thanks go to Terry Barker, editorial consultant and proofreader, for his tireless help, and to Katherine L. Gordon for her proofreading and moral support. I must also acknowledge the encouragement I received from the late Norma West Linder during this long process. Completion of this anthology would have been difficult without her by my side.

I also wish to mention my debt to Dr. David Bentley, the Carl F. Klinck Professor of Canadian Literature at Western University, for making long out-of-print books available via the internet and for his Canadian Poetry Project. He has kept Confederation poetry alive in our digital age.

Finally, it is my deep pleasure to thank Michael Mirolla, Connie McParland, Elana Wolff, David Moratto, Julie Roorda, and the entire team at Guernica Editions for their faith in my editing, their excellent book design, and for providing my beloved literary home, my safe harbour.

Acknowledgments

About the Editor

James Deahl was born in Pittsburgh during 1945, and grew up in that city as well as in and around the Laurel Highlands of the Appalachian Mountains. He moved to Canada in 1970. For the past eighteen years he has been a full-time writer, editor, and translator. He is the author or editor of over thirty books (mostly poetry) and is the author of fifteen poetry chapbooks. His previous Guernica poetry collections are *Travelling The Lost Highway*, *Red Haws To Light The Field*, and *Rooms The Wind Makes*. A cycle of his poems is the focus of a one-hour television special, *Under The Watchful Eye*. (Both the video and an audiotape of this program have been reissued on DVD and CD by Silver Falls Video.) While employed by TVOntario, he was the project leader and senior writer for the ten-part educational series *The Academy on Canadian Literature*. As a literary critic, Deahl has written about Milton Acorn, Raymond Souster, and Bruce Meyer, and he has lectured on Alden Nowlan, Robert Kroetsch, Canadian Postmodernism, and on the People's Poetry tradition.

This anthology is the companion volume to *The Confederation Poets: The Founding of a Canadian Poetry, 1880 to the First World War*, also from Guernica. Having lived in Ottawa, Almonte, Sudbury, Wanup, Toronto, London, and Hamilton, James Deahl now makes his home in Sarnia, Ontario. He is the father of three daughters: Sarah, Simone, and Shona, with whom he is translating into English the selected poems of Émile Nelligan. He is the grandfather of Scot and Felix.

Printed by Imprimerie Gauvin
Gatineau, Québec